PENGUIN BOOKS

REBELS, TRAITORS, PEACEMAKERS: TRUE STORIES OF LOVE AND CONFLICT IN INDIAN-CHINESE RELATIONSHIPS

Shivaji Das is the author of six critically acclaimed travel, art and business books. He was the first prize winner for Time Magazine's Sub-Continental Drift Essay contest and shortlisted for Fair Australia Prize for Short Stories.

Shivaji has been actively involved in migrant issues and is the conceptualiser and organiser for the acclaimed Migrant Worker and Refugee Poetry Contests in Singapore, Malaysia and Kenya and is the founder and director of the Global Migrant Festival (https://www.globalmigrantfestival.com/).

Shivaji's work and his interviews have been featured on BBC, CNBC, The Economist, Travel Radio Australia, Around the World TV, etc. Shivaji's writings have been published in magazines such as TIME, Nikkei, South China Morning Post, Think China, Asian Geographic, Jakarta Post, Conscious Magazine, PanaJournal, Freethinker, etc.

Shivaji Das was born and brought up in the northeastern province of Assam in India. Shivaji is a graduate from IIT Delhi and has an MBA from IIM Calcutta. He works as the Managing Director-APAC for Frost & Sullivan, a research and consulting company. Shivaji is currently a Singapore citizen. https://www.shivajidas.com

Yolanda Yu is the author of *Neighbour's Luck*, a collection of short stories that was shortlisted for the Singapore Literature Award 2020. She has received multiple literary awards, including DIX MOTS short story award by Alliance Francaise, Golden Point Award 2017 and 2015, and Singapore Tertiary

Chinese Literature Award 2001. Yolanda's work has been featured in Singapore Writers' Festival, various anthologies and magazines and newspapers such as LianHeZaoBao (Singapore), Cha Journal (Hong Kong), New York Times Travel, Zuopin Magazine and Guangxi Literature Magazine (China).

Yolanda is a co-organiser for Singapore Migrant Worker Poetry Contest and Global Migrant Festival, and an event host and coordinator for outreach for the Chinese migrant worker community. Yolanda volunteered at AWARE (Association of Women for Action & Research) as a help-liner and represented the organisation in a youth education program on Channel-U. She has interviewed people below the poverty line in Singapore as a volunteer for "Daughters of Tomorrow" and conducted a writing workshop for sex workers and the transgender community with ProjectX.

Born in North-Eastern China, Yolanda came to Singapore on scholarship in 1998 and has been living there since then. She holds a Computer Science degree from the National University of Singapore and an MBA from INSEAD Business School. After 20 years of corporate career, Yolanda is now an Executive Coach for career and leadership development.

Shivaji Das and Yolanda Yu have co-authored another book titled *The Visible Invisibles: Stories of migrant workers in Asia*, published by Penguin Random House SEA, 2022.

ADVANCE PRAISE FOR
REBELS, TRAITORS, PEACEMAKERS

'This book casts a timely spotlight on the dynamics of Indian–Chinese mixed marriages, mostly between Indian men and Chinese women. Of necessary microscopic detail, it opens a significant window into such marriages from the inside out, as partners speak out about their experiences and challenges not just between themselves but between their families and the society at large. An important resource for scholars, and a highly readable book for the curious in the increasingly multiracial, multicultural societies we live in.'

—Saras Manickam,
Winner of the 2019 Commonwealth
Short Story Prize (Asia)

Also by Shivaji Das and Yolanda Yu

The Visible Invisibles (2023)

'The power of love is that it sees all people.'

—DaShanne Stokes

'It is time for parents to teach young people early on that in diversity there is beauty and there is strength.'

—Maya Angelou

'. . . Ask yourself this question. If your child brings back a boyfriend or a girlfriend of a different race, will you be delighted? I will answer you frankly. I do not think I will. I may eventually accept it. So it is deep in the psyche of a human being.'

—Lee Kuan Yew

Rebels, Traitors, Peacemakers

True Stories of Love and Conflict in Indian-Chinese Relationships

Shivaji Das and Yolanda Yu

PENGUIN BOOKS

An imprint of Penguin Random House

PENGUIN BOOKS

USA | Canada | UK | Ireland | Australia
New Zealand | India | South Africa | China | Southeast Asia

Penguin Books is part of the Penguin Random House group of companies
whose addresses can be found at global.penguinrandomhouse.com

Published by Penguin Random House SEA Pte Ltd
9, Changi South Street 3, Level 08-01,
Singapore 486361

First published in Penguin Books by Penguin Random House SEA 2024
Copyright © Shivaji Das and Yolanda Yu 2024

ISBN 9789815127140

Typeset in Adobe Caslon Pro by MAP Systems, Bengaluru, India
Printed at Markono Print Media Pte Ltd, Singapore

www.penguin.sg

Contents

Introduction

In our twelve years together as a Chinese–Indian couple, we have often received both curious and annoyed glances. Is it because we are rare? Or because we are disrupting social codes? Other such couples were less fortunate than us. In 2022, a man in Singapore allegedly spat towards an Indian–Chinese couple and said, ' . . . you shouldn't be with a Chinese girl . . . that should be my girl.'[1]

17 per cent of all marriages in the USA in 2019 were between people of different races or ethnicities, up from just 3 per cent in 1967.[2] In Singapore, nearly one in five marriages is interracial. Indian–Chinese relationships also follow this general pattern for interracial coupling, with an increasing number of individuals from these two cultures choosing to marry and build families together. However, despite the growing prevalence of interracial relationships, interracial couples often experience discrimination or mistreatment because of their relationship.[3]

---

[1] Fiona Tan, 'Man allegedly spits on interracial couple at Orchard Central', *Mothership*, December 26, 2022, https://mothership.sg/2022/12/man-spit-interracial-couple-orchard/

[2] Livingston, Gretchen and Anna Brown, 'Intermarriage in the U.S. 50 years after Loving v. Virginia', *Pew Research Center* (2017).

[3] Midy, Tarah, 'The examination of discrimination and social bias toward interracial relationships', *Binghamton University Graduate Dissertations and Theses* (2018).

In the context of Chinese–Indian relationships, these challenges are further compounded by historical and political factors that have created cultural biases and stereotypes. The ongoing border dispute and tense relationship between India and China also affect cultural attitudes towards their respective citizens and diaspora. And despite there being nearly three billion Chinese and Indian people, limited direct exposure to each other has bred racism as seen by the mutual name-calling of one another as uncultured, unhygienic, backward, untrustworthy, contagious, and dangerous.

Yet, in the midst of these complications, there are stories of people who have found love and forged new relationships that transcend cultural and geopolitical boundaries. Their stories are both heart-warming and heart-wrenching, as they reveal these couples' courage and determination to follow their hearts, even in the face of opposition, often from their loved ones.

What—amidst all the macro-tensions—bonds such couples together? What magnetic forces make them persevere? What insights do such unusual unions reveal about broader human nature?

This book, *Rebels, Traitors, Peacemakers: True Stories of Love and Conflict in Indian–Chinese Relationships*, dwells on these questions through the lives of thirty-two individuals— including us—involved in such relationships. Set across Singapore, Malaysia, China, Canada, Australia, India, the United Kingdom, Nepal, and the United States, these individuals are rebels who defy cultural norms and expectations. They are the 'traitors', sometimes labelled as 'spies', who face the disapproval and rejection of their families and communities. And they are also peacemakers who find ways to reconcile their differences and create a new identity.

This book, however, is not just about the struggles involved in Indian–Chinese relationships. Beyond documenting the weddings and break-ups, similarities and differences, smiles and tears, likes and dislikes, these stories dwell on how we see the world and how we are seen. As such, this book is also an exploration of what makes us human and how religious contexts, cultural heritage, racism, societal expectations, intergenerational power play, minority-majority status, and political tensions trickle down to our day-to-day lives. These real, unsweetened stories of the featured individuals pose several questions: How much of difference emanates from cultural backgrounds and how much from individual personality characteristics? Can alternate identities such as religion wipe out Indian-ness or Chinese-ness completely? Do certain life experiences predestine people for intercultural relationships? How strong is the power of domestication in removing all traces of cultural differences? Can culture become a convenient excuse for transgressions?

The featured individuals have been chosen to provide a balanced mix: across countries where they live, their socio-economic status, sexual orientation, relationship status, etc. Their stories are laced with experiences that tread on the edge of the tragic and the comic: linguistic faux pas, shock at alien food habits, cultural misunderstandings, and bigoted reactions from strangers. Finer details of the cultural practices of the two population groups reveal striking similarities—filial piety, obsessive ambition, and a permanent sense of inferiority on the world stage. Because of the unique choices they have made, the featured characters clearly demonstrate the human qualities of adaptability, rebelliousness, and resoluteness. Yet, by also showcasing their frustrations, guilt, and doubts, the collection unearths the collateral damages experienced when the lives of people from two great civilizations collide.

The stories have been largely presented as told by the featured individuals, with edits for clarity, consistency, and flow. All views presented in this book are only those of the featured individuals. These stories have been organized as per common themes with substantial overlaps between them. For conversations conducted in languages other than English, we have translated them ourselves. For those concerned about revealing their identities, we have used pseudonyms or aliases, often chosen by the concerned individual. We have, in particular, been cautious about not masking over real challenges in such relationships.

Certain commonalities emerge from the diversity of the presented stories. The featured individuals exhibit personality traits—openness, curiosity, rationality, rebelliousness, and resoluteness—that perhaps drive them to be in interracial relationships. They have to overcome significant opposition from their own families, which is expected given the conservative patriarchal nature of both Indian and Chinese cultures. The women suffer the most, to the extent of being locked up and beaten by their family members. Their partners face frequent insults. Outsiders, however, have limited influence, their reaction limited to the occasional stare, a passing comment, or some online trolling. The couples overcome their family's resistance with their persistence, patience, logical arguments, creativity, and support from friends and relatives. Once the relationship is formally sealed, this familial opposition wilts rapidly. The cultural differences, too, cede ground—while never entirely leaving the scene—to individual personality traits causing the couples to have highs and lows like any other. Certain unique practical challenges such as communication issues and matching up to societal expectations do linger on. While interracial couples, in general, have been documented to have a higher rate of separation than average,[4] the Indian–

---

[4] 'The Rise of Intermarriage: Rates, Characteristics Vary by Race and Gender', *Pew Social & Demographic Trends* (2012).

Chinese couples seem to stick together—a characteristic (fidelity and loyalty) often cited by one to praise the other. But if separation does happen, racial biases against the other race can creep in. Those who have stayed together, though, harbour no regrets. Despite concerns about the potential bullying their children may face, most couples feel positive about the future of their mixed next generation. Overall, they view their relationship as a positive message to the world—an expression of a desire for mutual understanding and shared humanity.

If love and conflict are two sides of the same coin, nowhere is this more evident than in Indian–Chinese relationships. Ultimately, this book is about the power of love to transform our lives and communities. Through these stories of Indian–Chinese relationships, we are reminded of the importance of empathy, understanding, and acceptance in bridging cultural differences, as well as the easy temptation of falling for stereotypes. Our goal in writing this book will be achieved if these stories inspire readers to challenge cultural stereotypes and biases and embrace the diversity and richness of our world while firmly endorsing the reaffirming qualities of human life.

It was our privilege and honour to record these life journeys.

Yolanda Yu, Shivaji Das
March 2023, Singapore

I

Can we explain what triggers love? Coincidences, chance encounters, unforeseen chains of events, inexplicable attraction—in the context of Indian–Chinese relationships, pinpointing that transformative moment from being mere acquaintances to making a lifelong commitment can be even more elusive. Their stories, then, appear even more 'unbelievable.'

And yet, from the enchantment of love at first sight to the pragmatic considerations of choosing a life partner, interracial couples traverse a similar spectrum of emotions as happens in any other relationship. And despite the inevitable nit-picking, when an ocean stands as a barrier, their love can reveal a heroic nature.

Our Unbelievable Story

The story of Nitin Masih, thirties, Indian and Luo Feiyang (Luoluo), thirties, Chinese. They are married and live in Chongqing, China.

Nitin: We have an unbelievable story. I never planned to live outside India. I love my mother so much. I can't live without her. And yet, I have been living in China, away from her, for three years, ever since we got married.

I was born in Udaipur—the 'White City'—in North India. I'm a Christian. In our town, Hindus, Muslims, and Christians live together harmoniously. We don't even lock our houses there.

My father died when I was young. So I had to support my family soon after graduating from intermediate school. I worked in a call centre in New Delhi for two years. But my mother and I then decided that I should study further. With a cousin's help, I went to Bangkok for a Hotel Management course. The person in charge ran away, taking our school fees. Thankfully, with some help from friends and family, I managed to enter another university programme. After graduation, I worked as an intern at the Asia Hotel, one of the oldest hotels in Bangkok. I was their first foreign staff. I won the management's love and was soon promoted to Duty Manager.

When my would-be wife came to stay at the Asia Hotel, I was the shift manager of the day. I wasn't at the reception desk but I could see her checking in. I felt some good vibes. I became attracted to her. She went to her room without noticing me. Later that night, I saw her again at the front desk. She was complaining about her room light. I had already completed my shift and was about to leave. I also had a flight the next morning, to go home for Christmas. But the manager for the night shift was having dinner and the housekeeping was overwhelmed. So, they called upon me to check things out. I followed her to her room. I still remember her room number—425. She had gotten the worst room in the hotel!

I couldn't fix the light, so I had to call the housekeeper. But I lingered around in her room till everything was settled. Then I gave her my name card and left. I flew home the next day.

Suddenly, I received a text in Chinese. It was her, thanking me for the help. I was delighted. Few guests show appreciation for our work. They see it as our duty. I replied, 'You are welcome.'

I connected with her on WeChat. My first message there was to ask how her room was. Slowly, we started talking.

Luoluo: I knew it was him when I got the WeChat invite. He had already 'harassed' me many times by then! After I checked in at the hotel, he stalked me at the lift and shop entrances to chat me up. I kept using different entrances to avoid 'chancing upon' him. But somehow, he would always be on my way. And yet, I didn't mind his 'harassment' [laughs].

I always had many men around me. Arrogant as I was, I didn't like any of them. Once I reached thirty, my parents started chasing me to get married. But I was not even dating. Where could I find a man to marry? Every year, I travelled overseas around my birthday, so I could escape from my parent's nagging. I worked in the property sector. The market then was good, and I made decent money. I used that income to travel around Southeast Asia. Thailand was my favourite because of its thrilling shopping. I could take BTS[5] anywhere in Bangkok and visit the night markets.

I met Nitin on one such trip. He looked neither Thai nor European. It never crossed my mind that he might be an Indian. I had no idea about India anyway. The country was so mysterious. I thought he was Middle Eastern. Later I would joke that I talked to him only because I thought he was from Dubai.

Nitin: She couldn't speak English, I couldn't speak Chinese. But thanks to the translation function on WeChat, we could talk. We talked every day. I talk a lot anyway. I would start some conversation and if I didn't receive any reply, I would ask a new question to which she had to reply. She felt touched by my daily greetings.

Luoluo: He used to call me thirty–forty times a day. When someone asks you daily 'Have you eaten?', 'How was your sleep?' it almost becomes a habit. Slowly, I opened up to him. Once he showed me on Google Maps that Chongqing Yubei district—my location—was near north-eastern India, as if we were neighbours. I have never met anyone as persistent as him. I had always found it hard to trust others. But his persistence made me trust him. How strange!

Nitin: I was not just looking for fun. I was looking for someone I could trust and have a family with. So, I got serious. In 2017, I visited her in Chongqing. And then we met again in Bangkok. I also introduced her to my mother over a video call.

We ran into conflict when my work became heavy. This was when I had to work eighteen-hour shifts because my manager became paralysed. I was always tired. I slept whenever

---

[5] Subway in Bangkok.

I found some time. I couldn't talk much to her then. She was understanding. But her friends seeded doubts in her mind.

Luoluo: My friends suggested that 'the foreigner' had some other girl. I had no way to verify. Many times, I wanted to give up. I deleted him from WeChat. But he always managed to come back. Thanks to his thick skin, we stayed together.

I had never wanted a long-distance relationship, not even with someone in Beijing, or Chengdu (a city near Chongqing). And yet, I ended up in a long-distance relationship with someone based so far away. How strange. I often told him I felt short-changed—he was a namesake boyfriend who couldn't even pass me a cup of water when I fell sick.

He started looking for jobs for me in Thailand. But I only wanted to go to Thailand for holidays, not for work. I was doing well in the property market in Chongqing. So I told him, 'Stop wasting my time, let's just part ways.'

Nitin: I had to make a decision. I could find other jobs, but I wouldn't find this girl again. So I left my job and went to India for the necessary documents. Three months later, I was in Chongqing to marry her.

Luoluo: Everyone in his family—his brother, sister and brother-in-law—was against him marrying a Chinese. As a Chinese, I think highly of ourselves. So I never expected Indians to not like Chinese. They said that if he married an Indian girl, his wife could take care of the mom. I was shocked at this logic. Why can't his siblings take care of the mom? Why would everything be on his wife? Why would even a brother-in-law have a say in his marriage? I couldn't understand anything. It turned out that a brother-in-law is of high status in Indian families. And his brother-in-law worked in the US which added more weight.

But his mom supported him. She told him to quit his job and go to China. My mom-in-law played an important role in our marriage. She is a wise woman. She probably imagined him marrying a foreigner anyway when she sent him to study overseas.

I respect his mom a lot. She was among the first women from North-Eastern India to receive an English education. She speaks better English than me. She is very open-minded, more than many of our Chinese parents. She worked hard to get my hubby and his siblings educated in private schools.

His coming to China to marry me was no easy task. Looking at the documents he needed for international marriage, I couldn't believe he could get it done. It took him over three months in India to get these done. But when he came to China, he was still pending the Single Certificate. If we went with the 'Indian speed,' this document would have expired by the time he got it. So his mom employed an agent to expedite this.

When I told my dad about him, he was shocked. He said, 'Play all you like. But don't play so big. Find someone nearby. A foreigner? Nonsense.' He stopped talking to me, his usual reaction when he couldn't handle something. He thought I would 'recover' over time. But I didn't. I have always been very independent. I went to boarding school. Since a very young age, I have made my own decisions.

My mom liked Nitin. She thought he looked good. He was fashionable and had a well-toned body. He cares about his image a lot. Even when he had to get up early in the Thailand hotel, he would wash and style his hair daily. She also thought he was reliable because he came to China for me. Eventually, my dad also accepted our relationship.

Other people were shocked to hear about us. My relatives—those who knew about India—thought it was the poorest country in the world. How could you marry someone from there? Others kept confusing India with Africa. I corrected them many times. But they still went on to tell people that my husband was African. Well, they live in the villages. They don't know. I also had this strange arrogance before meeting Nitin. But now I have learned about the outside world: While India and China look down on each other, the developed countries look down on both. How strange of us to think that we are the centre of the world!

Because of COVID-19, we couldn't have a proper wedding. We just got the registration done. My parents were disappointed. His mom was too. She had dreamt of having a week-long wedding in India. I had freaked out hearing the number of guests she was planning for. We also had plans to have a church wedding in Bangkok.

We have been married for a few years now. People will find it strange if we hold any ceremonies at this point. Maybe we can host something once we have kids, to make up for the plans we all had.

It wasn't easy for Nitin to settle down after our marriage. He didn't have a job. Chongqing is not a tourist city, so the hotel industry salary here is pathetic. I wouldn't let him work on those terms. This troubled him. We quarrelled a lot.

With him, I get angry easily. Compared to Chinese boys, he is too direct. He would say, 'You are becoming fat,' 'You are looking old.' He has learned to apologize profusely whenever he says something nasty like that, but his behaviour hasn't changed completely.

We speak English when we are all fine. But when we are angry, English runs away somewhere. He will throw Hindi and Thai at me. I will throw my Chongqing Chinese. But I know the Hindi curse words, and he knows mine. In any case, you don't need to understand the language when fighting. The tones are sufficient.

But I knew where his sadness came from. He was well established in Thailand. He studied there, had many friends, and had a well-paying job. He gave up so much for me. But I couldn't do much for him. Every day, I still had to leave the house for work. Only our dogs could give him company.

Nitin: My wife cares for me whenever I feel depressed or short-tempered. She showed me around Chongqing. She reminded me of my sister in India, who always cares for the family. Luoluo's love for animals made me emotional—especially how she cared for street dogs and street cats. I had never liked dogs before. Today we have three dogs. She adopted these abandoned dogs. One of them was so special. I cry whenever I talk about her [tearful]. I only had her for one whole day. That day, whenever Luoluo and I argued, this dog would try to stop us from fighting. The next day, she died of stomach cancer . . . She taught me about real emotions. She changed my heart.

Later, I found a job teaching kids English online. I didn't mind the low pay; it was only ¥5,000. I just wanted to work.

Luoluo: Indians are talkative and sharp-mouthed. They have a baffling confidence. He is always right, I am always wrong. He is tidy. He folds every cloth neatly. But I am lazy. When we just got together, he folded my clothes too. But now, he has become lazy like me [laughs]. He loves shopping; I am too lazy now for that. Nowadays, he shops for my clothes and I just wear whatever he picks. His taste is not bad. And if he buys something, it means he likes me dressed that way. So I just wear it.

And I don't regret our marriage at all.

Nitin: I have fallen in love with Chongqing and its people. I have never faced any discrimination here. I feel safe in Chongqing, and unlike in India, I have never seen any fights here. India can learn many things from China, especially on safety.

Luoluo: Nitin loves our Chongqing food. Our food is spicy so we can fight Chongqing's humid weather. On rainy days, he craves our spicy hotpot. Because Nitin is Christian, he has no food restrictions like many other Indians. But we do go to Indian restaurants whenever he misses his hometown food.

There was this one time we ate octopus limbs in a Korean restaurant. We posted the pictures in the family group chat. His mom was shocked—how can such food be healthy? And during the pandemic, she would always ask us to avoid pork; she believes that pork carries the virus.

In Bangkok, Nitin used to go to church every week. But in Chongqing, he never asked about it. After we got married, his mother asked him to get me baptized. I didn't mind. I knew it wouldn't affect me in any way. As Nitin rightly says, we Chinese only have one belief—to make money. The church nearest to my place is far, though. So we rarely go there.

Nitin: I do feel sad because I can't go home. I have been here since 2019. Now the world is free, people can go anywhere. But in China, the COVID-19 restrictions are still very strict. I don't dare to leave, fearing that I can't come back in. She will be here alone then. I am just waiting for China to open again.

Luoluo: He talks to his mom every day. In China, we don't call our parents so often, only during festivals or when something comes up. I wouldn't have much to say even if I was sitting next to my mom. But he tells his mom anything and everything—something happened in his school, our dogs met cats downstairs. She knew even if he felt itchy somewhere. Earlier, I would be shocked. Now I find it normal. I have got used to his talkativeness. I also hear the same thing from other Chinese wives with Indian husbands. Maybe Indians have the close ties we lack, though a tad too much?

Earlier, I had insisted on living in China. I feel safer in my own country. But the country's COVID-19 response has disappointed many. Now I am open to living anywhere, even in India.

It's much easier for me to get OCI[6] in India than for him to get a spouse visa in China. He only gets a one-year visitor visa and must keep renewing it every year. But one American friend of mine got a three-year visa easily. The person is less educated than my husband. Perhaps this is because of political tensions between China and India. The two countries have no big issues but are never short of small ones.

I have never been to India. I had a terrible impression of the country. But in my mum-in-law's photos, India appears very clean. His childhood photos remind me of mine. It could be because of their social class. My friends who live in India also tell me it's developing fast because of the demographic dividend. That sounds like China ten years ago. If India offers good opportunities, I will be happy to move there. Then he can be with his mom. He came all the way to China for me, I can also go all the way to India for him.

---

[6] Overseas Citizen of India.

II

The 'family' is the invincible Himalayan frontier for Chinese–Indian romantic relationships. With both cultures having strong conservative and patriarchal undertones, codified expectations of the ideal son-in-law or the ideal daughter-in-law collide with massive consequences, especially for the women in the relationship. Some are locked up, some are beaten. Their partners are frequently insulted. In addition, these relationships bear witness to hidden currents of racism, casteism, and the open influence of religion, often creating a toxic atmosphere with the menacing fear—what will others think?

But if distance breeds suspicion, does proximity increase trust? Even in cosmopolitan societies like Singapore where the two communities live closely, the social dynamics of majority vs minority groups play out in complicated ways. This incomplete familiarity with the 'other' reinforces negative biases when one's own child finds a partner outside the race. Family members then go to the extent of disowning them. Your own child then becomes not only a rebel, but also a traitor—not just to the family but to the entire race.

What, can then, bring about a resolution? How can such couples cross the Himalayas, together? Is it just patience, time, perseverance or does it need to be a well-planned escape?

The Big Explosion of Curry
and Dumplings

The story of Dr Rebecca Yip Ghosh, thirties, British–Chinese, and Arnav Ghosh, thirties, Indian. They are married and live in Edinburgh, Scotland.

Rebecca: I grew up in Bristol, England. My parents moved there from Hong Kong, but they went back when I was sixteen. For a while, I was living in the UK by myself until I joined my parents in Hong Kong when I went there for my PhD. There, I met Arnav.

It was difficult growing up as a Chinese person in the UK. Where we lived, almost everyone was white. I didn't feel like I belonged there. I was bullied a lot. Sometimes, the other kids would say, 'Go back to your own country.' It got better as I grew older. Or I just developed a thicker skin. My parents didn't integrate much with British society either. My dad had migrated to the UK along with his siblings and other people from the same village. They remained a closed group, mingling mostly among themselves, hardly interacting with others.

But it wasn't easy for me in Hong Kong either. I was too 'white' to be Hong Kong-ish but also very Chinese to be British. I couldn't adapt to some aspects of local culture. Like, seniority is such a big deal in Hong Kong. But while I respect everyone, it feels weird when someone demands respect just because of age.

So I couldn't wait to leave. I heard the 'Chinkie' thing a lot while growing up in the UK. And in Hong Kong, locals would call me 'banana'—yellow outside but white on the inside.

But now that I've left Hong Kong for Scotland, I want to return to Hong Kong. I am caught between the two worlds.

Arnav: My parents are both Bengali but I grew up in Delhi, and I consider myself a Delhiite. Just from the way I speak Hindi, someone can tell that I am so.

I came to study in Hong Kong when I was eighteen. It was a shock—an entirely new life. I come from a middle-class family, which in India means that the father is a salaried man and the mother is a housewife. So back home, I always had someone to help me with things—someone to make food or help me with homework. I didn't even know how to do my laundry. But when I moved to Hong Kong, I had to do everything.

Moreover, I didn't know anyone there. I was not used to the food. I didn't speak the language, even the teachers spoke to the students in Cantonese if I was not involved. It was terrible. I wanted to go back home even before the first semester was over.

In Hong Kong, I did face some racism. There, if you have gone to an international school, you have international friends and are open to immigrants. But if you're very local and have only lived in a Hong Kong kind of bubble, you don't like outsiders. So I got dirty looks from some. If I was sitting on the metro or bus, some would leave the seat next to me empty. They said we Indians are smelly. Even some Hong Kong-born Indians wouldn't want to hang out with me. It's like, since I'm Hong Kong born and you are India born, you're different—the same happens with Indians in the UK too.

But it was better once I made some friends there. They taught me some Cantonese, especially the swear words. After that, I could integrate better. And I could tell if people were abusing me behind my back; I would then confront them. So, I decided to stay. I stayed for nine years. And even now, I can't do without Hong Kong food.

Rebecca: Arnav and I were at the same university in Hong Kong. This was back in 2014. Both of us had joined this Facebook group for international students. And I knew a lot of other Indian PhD students, some of whom knew Arnav and said he was great. So, we got talking on Messenger and WhatsApp, and we formed a good bond. He also had a very nice profile picture on Facebook.

One day, some of us from that Facebook group planned to meet up. I messaged everyone before the meet-up to confirm, but no one replied. On that day, just the two of us turned up. The others said later that they just wanted to give us a chance to meet alone. Looking back, it worked out.

Arnav: I was fresh out of a breakup. I just wanted to meet new people. I came across her YouTube channel called 'Asian Chem Nerd' and found it very interesting. I thought I would love to meet this person. And then it just happened. Bex and I met in mid-August, and by mid-September, we were dating. It was all so quick. But it was all very natural.

Rebecca: I had never expected to end up with an Indian. I always imagined that I would eventually have a regular Chinese family—just like my parents—even when I had a white boyfriend. In Hong Kong, some local boys were interested in me. I debated whether I should go with someone I was attracted to but who wasn't Chinese. Earlier, I had a long-term relationship with another British-born Chinese. He didn't speak any Cantonese. He wasn't very close to his family either. This wasn't how I imagined British–Chinese families to be. With him, I saw how bad a relationship could be. Our communication was terrible. I got gaslighted whenever I raised something I was unhappy about. I was always manipulated into apologizing even though it was me who was unhappy to begin with. So back then, I just shut myself down.

But with Arnav, all these bad things weren't happening. Our communication was so much better. We felt free to talk through everything. Our values are very similar. We're both aspirational, always striving for more—I don't like people who are just content with staying put. We're both very close to our families, which was important to me. It was difficult to bond with the earlier guy's family, they were not trusting. But Arnav's family treats me like a daughter. So, this ideal I had in my head of a perfect relationship with a Chinese guy who was also British—just like me—ended up so differently. That's what made me go for Arnav.

Arnav: After my previous partner, an Indonesian–Chinese girl, cheated on me, I thought that I was not going to be with a Chinese girl ever again. It was a traumatic experience. But life doesn't work like that. I began to think that just as I don't want people to discriminate against me as an Indian because they might have had a bad experience with some other Indian, I can't completely reject all Chinese girls because of one sour experience. I tried to see it fairly. It was not about a race, it was about a person.

I got along so well with Bex. And while Bex is Chinese, she speaks fluent English. We would just talk and talk and that's how we built a bond. I found her very cool because of her videos. She wanted to return to the UK, which worked for me. I wanted to be in a place where language wouldn't be a constraint. My parents also liked her. When they came to know that she was doing her PhD, they were so impressed. So everything added up and now, we are here.

Rebecca: At first, my parents were okay with our relationship. But things changed once they met him for the first time. Earlier, I had told them that my boyfriend is Indian, but he speaks Cantonese. Maybe I exaggerated how good Arnav's Cantonese was. The reality was that Arnav spoke only 'survival Cantonese'. So when my parents eventually met him, they couldn't have a full conversation. My parents said, 'Oh, his Cantonese isn't that good.' It was my fault that their expectations were set so high.

Arnav: Honestly, back then, I had a very low level of Cantonese. It has gotten better with time—I'm learning all the time from her parents when they are here. But she oversold me to her parents to overcome their prejudice.

Rebecca: Getting my parents to accept Arnav became a long and uphill battle after that meeting. They worried that Indian men were chauvinistic and their wives had no rights. They said my PhD would be wasted because I would become a stay-at-home mom and I would not have a say in anything. This perception of Indians came from the UK media. In the eighties and nineties, if an Indian family made it to the news there, it was only because some husband had beaten up his wife or someone was forced into an arranged marriage.

My parents never said 'no' explicitly until we had this huge argument. That was the milestone. Arnav and I had moved in together in a rented apartment in Hong Kong. He was still studying while working part-time. Then Arnav lost his job, so we both moved into my parents' house. That created many issues. Hong Kong houses are small. There were now four people in there. Yet, I had assumed that we would get along easily because of our common Asian culture and that my parents would make Arnav feel at home. But for Arnav, 'feel at home' meant how it was at his home where his mom did everything for him, and he didn't have to lift a finger. In our home, it was the opposite. The kids do everything for the parents. The elders are the most important. Whereas in his family, the kids are the most important. So that's what Arnav assumed when my parents said, 'Feel at home.' And when he did, my parents were not happy.

It was just a matter of time before things blew up. There was much struggle. Many arguments. I felt it was not going to work out. And it all exploded on that milestone day. My mom had wanted Arnav to pay rent. Arnav gave whatever he could. My mother—forever the penny pincher—wasn't happy. That evening, when I came home, my mum made a snide comment about Arnav. She said, 'Is this all he is giving?' I listened, went straight into the bedroom, stood on top of the bed, and began crying, absolutely howling.

I was so tired of all this. I couldn't take the stress of being the mediator between my parents and Arnav any longer. Then Arnav also stood on top of the bed and tried to calm me down, not understanding what was going on. Because it's Hong Kong, the walls are thin, so my parents heard me crying and Arnav talking. They thought that Arnav had done something to me. They burst in. And then everyone was shouting. My mom screamed, 'What are you doing to my daughter?' I was crying my eyes out, so I couldn't say anything. Arnav shouted at my mom, 'You know, you are the cause of this'. Then my mom said, 'I want you out of my house.' I think that was the best English she's ever spoken.

Hearing that, I said, 'Fine, we are leaving. We're leaving this house right now.' I said to Arnav, 'Come on, let's go.' Arnav said, 'What's going on?' My dad was the only one asking everyone to calm down. He took me out of the house and stood at the bus stop down the street. He asked me, 'Are you really going to let this break up the family? The only thing we want is for you to be happy, and we're just worried that this relationship isn't going to keep you happy. We're worried about him not treating you well. We're worried that you will not be able to do the things that you want to do.'

I explained to my father that I was actually very happy and that all of the things they thought were issues were not there. I told him that there was much miscommunication. For instance, my parents thought that Arnav never treated me to anything. But if we had told them we went for a hundred-dollar dinner, they'd have said, 'Oh, you're wasting so much money.' That's how Chinese parents are; they always want to save money. So we always told them that the things we did were very cheap. And they took it to imply that Arnav never did anything for me. Either way, we can't win.

When we returned to the house, my mom said, 'It's fine. You can have this relationship, but I'll forget that I have a daughter, and you can forget about me being your mother.' I said, 'I don't want that. I want our family to be happy, but I also want you to realize that I'm happy in my relationship.' Then we hugged. I went to Arnav and said, 'I'd appreciate it if you apologize to my mom for shouting at her.' He apologized. That helped. Everything just got better from that point.

Maybe we needed that explosion to happen. Everyone had just been holding back their thoughts. So, we just needed to let it out and talk properly. Soon after, Arnav got a job. We moved out of the house, and things got even better. Sometimes, Arnav treated my parents. Sometimes, he gave money to my grandma. My mother boasted about these to all other family members. She made a big deal out of such things.

Arnav: Everything was fine by the time we got married. We also didn't have any issues because of our religious differences. Bex doesn't have a religion but doesn't mind going to a temple. Her family is also very open when it comes to such matters. They are not particularly religious but have Buddhist values. My family is Hindu. I grew up as a Hindu, and I identify as a Hindu. Yet, I don't restrict myself from eating certain kinds of meat because of my religion. My parents are okay with it even though they are strict vegetarians. If my mom hears about me eating beef, she will say, 'Oh my god, what is my son eating? What a shame. Are you even my son?' But she is still fine with me.

We had two weddings—the registry wedding in Hong Kong and a Bengali-style wedding in India. My parents insisted on us having a proper traditional Hindu-Bengali wedding. It was stressful because weddings in India can get out of hand. More than a hundred people were invited. So many things happened over three days—*Haldi*, dances, many rituals—it was all very tiring. Everybody wanted to take Bex's picture. It was overwhelming. On the wedding day, I had to put on this ugly-looking crown which every Bengali groom must wear. All my life, I had been saying that I would never wear that at my wedding. But they put it on my head anyway. It is the least sexy thing a man can wear.

Bex's parents also came to India for the wedding. Our parents had never met each other until then. Anyway, it was too late to back out if they didn't like each other—sorry. In any case, my parents treated Bex very well. Everyone treated her very well. So it all went fine.

Now we even have our own YouTube Channel. There, we post videos about ourselves, to share how an Indian and Chinese couple can be together.

Rebecca: There are still big differences in how our respective families interact with us. Food-wise, for example. When Arnav's parents are with us, his mom cooks whatever each of us wants. One wants roti, one wants fried rice, and one wants paratha. And we all want to eat at different times. So his mom ends up cooking all day. I would say that you make whatever is convenient and whatever everyone else is eating. But she insists I make my own choice. I felt quite uncomfortable with this amount of accommodation that Arnav's parents do. Why is it always so flexible? Because this is not how I was raised. I ate what was given to me. So when my parents are here, it's the opposite. My dad cooks, and we all eat together, and that's it. Sometimes, Arnav doesn't want to eat that kind of food. That causes some tension. Food is my dad's love language. He loves to cook; he likes it if you eat his food and relish it. If you don't, he gets upset.

Arnav: Earlier, my mom used to ask, 'Does she eat snakes and frogs?' I would be angry hearing that. I would say, 'She could, but she doesn't. Not every Chinese person is just eating all things that move.' Even for me, I can't stand eating chicken feet; just the look of it. But it's such a delicacy in Asian culture. My wife loves it. I don't stop her, and she doesn't force me to eat it. But now my mother accepts Rebecca with a full heart.

Our parents from both sides spend a lot of time with our son, Aryan, and us. Bex's father stayed with us during her pregnancy, which was a massive help. He prepared traditional Chinese food like herbal soups for her. My parents also stay here for long periods. This has been very helpful because both of us are working. Grandparenting, obviously, is very personal. Everyone has their style. For example, Aryan is very independent even though he is only eighteen months old. He doesn't like to be fed even though the food spills everywhere when he tries to eat by himself. Since he was six months old, he has wanted his own bowl, spoon, and fork. But when our parents see the food spilling, they say, 'Why don't you just hold him and feed him?' Then, they want to take Aryan's spoon and feed him. That makes him angry. Then my parents would say, 'Oh my god, Aryan is very, very hard to manage.'

My parents want me to teach him Bengali. But it doesn't come so naturally to me. Bex's side speaks to Aryan in Cantonese. Bex and I speak to each other in English. And then we watch Korean dramas on Netflix. So Aryan is probably a bit confused. Maybe that's why he doesn't talk yet.

Rebecca: One of my biggest worries is that Aryan will be confused about who he is. He is Chinese, he is Indian, but he's also growing up in the UK. I'm still confused about who I am, so I worry he'll be even more confused.

Arnav: Our boy has an Indian name, Aryan. I do want to show him the Hindu culture from my side. I want to show him our festivals. So, we celebrate Hindu festivals like Diwali, Holi, and Durga Puja. We wear Indian clothes whenever we have to. But I don't care if he becomes a non-believer. He should just become a good person.

I want him to be able to relate to the Bengali side, but he should also be able to relate to being Chinese. But then we are in Scotland, so he is kind of Scottish. Scottish people don't relate with the British. He may be speaking to friends in a Scottish accent, very different from a typical British accent. He will be confused, right? Well, it's for him to navigate life the way he wants to.

But I do worry about how he will face the world and how the world will see him. Because while Indians and Chinese are the biggest races—a billion people each—they are also the two that get made fun of a lot and get many racial slurs. Certain connotations revolve around us. So, him being a mix of both, how will the world treat him? Recently, a colleague here, also a good friend, told me, 'Yo man, tell me why you don't smell, man? You don't smell like other Indians.' I said, 'I take showers, and you know, I have cologne and deodorants. I don't eat curry all day.' But Indians themselves can be so racist. They call people from the north-east 'chinkies', make fun of them and sometimes discriminate against them. So, India can be nice in many things, but it can also be weird. But I'm still proud to be an Indian. And I am proud that my son is half Chinese and half Indian.

Rebecca: Take our YouTube Channel, for example. With our Chinese Indian mix, we get a lot of racist comments like 'She's a spy cuz she's Chinese,' or 'If your wife is so nice, why did her Chinese people spread Covid?' I would take all such comments very personally. So now I don't even read the comments on our channel any more. Arnav curates all the comments.

Arnav: I've got a thick skin now regarding facing racism. I don't get offended any more, unlike everybody who gets offended these days by the slightest of things. So, our YouTube Channel is called 'Curry and Dumpling' because I'm curry, and she's dumpling. There is nothing to be ashamed of.

And now we realize that there are many like us. Our channel has grown from 700 to over 35,000 subscribers. Some comments are like, 'I'm also Chinese, and I have an Indian partner, and I have these struggles. Can you help us?' We write back long advice as comments. Everybody has their own circumstances. Every parent-child relationship is different. But we help where we can.

Yet, we eventually want to move back to Asia, somewhere like Singapore. Singapore is closer to where our parents live. Aryan would also integrate better there since Singapore has many more Chinese and Indians. Out here, even though it is very international, it's still very homogenous, very white. And we just miss the hustle and bustle of Asia in general.

I just hope that our son doesn't have to endure many negative things in life. I hope that in ten years, the world becomes more accepting and that being a mix is not as unseen as it used to be.

Is Race Really the Issue?

The story of Carmen Tan, twenties, Chinese-Singaporean, and Prateepan Varatharajullu, twenties, Indian Singaporean. Carmen lives in Singapore, while Prateepan lives in Ireland. Carmen and Prateepan are in a relationship.

Carmen: As a child, I didn't want to give my parents any problems. They already found my elder brother difficult; he was always rebellious. So my parents were very strict with him. To save them any more hassle, I mostly stayed at home, studied, and played computer games. I was very shy and didn't feel comfortable in big groups. I always hid behind my mom and followed her everywhere. I am an introvert. It still takes quite a while to get me talking. And then I met Prateepan. He was so sociable. He had such good energy. People just liked to hang around him.

We were only fourteen when we first met. Prateepan had joined the same school as me. We were at a birthday party of this common friend. The party was in a big room, and Prateepan was just playing with the PS4[7] he had brought along. I found it very weird, why would someone do that at a party? But then, he was so confident, he just didn't think of it as weird. He was playing,

---

[7] PlayStation 4, a video game console.

and then everyone gathered around him for some reason. Yeah. And so it just happened.

Prateepan: I am the youngest of four siblings, born many years after my parents had their third child. My mother worked as a teacher for over thirty years. She volunteered heavily in community services, organizing community events where she roped us kids in as well. Sometimes, we kids even had to run these events. So even as a child, I met many people and had many friends. Most were Chinese, which is natural because Singapore is 70–80 per cent Chinese.

At that party, I was watching a video, and Carmen sat beside me, and then she started laughing at the same thing as I did. She came across as such a sweet person. We just hit it off from there.

I had heard about Carmen before. But I never imagined that she'd be interested in me. I was the only Indian person at that party. So I just brushed off that day. I didn't want to think much about it. But she showed interest even after that, and I was like, okay, interesting. She said she needed help with maths, so I helped her. We started hanging out more; we began to study together.

Carmen: But we broke up soon. Prateepan used to come to my house often, just like my other friends. We studied together and sometimes watched movies together. One night, during our exam period, Prateepan was at my home, and my father suddenly appeared out of nowhere and said to him, 'I think it is time to leave.'

It was not what he said, but the way he said it.

Prateepan: Until that day, I had never felt unwelcome in Carmen's house. I visited often; she just lived down the street from my place. Her mother talked a lot to me whenever I came. But that day was different. Her father just stood there, staring at me, watching me pack. As I was walking back home, I felt so puzzled.

Carmen: Right after Prateepan left, my father told me that I couldn't be friends with him any more. He said that it was our time to focus on our studies. But why? My father never bothered me with anything before. I couldn't help but wonder if it was because Prateepan is Indian. My father never said anything about my Chinese male friends staying at home till even later. Why single out Prateepan then?

But then, my family never said anything bad about Indians. I never felt that they were racist or had any discrimination against others. I knew there was a sad practice where some Chinese parents in Singapore would warn their kids, 'Go to sleep; otherwise, Abu Nenne (a derogatory word for Indians) will come.' My parents never said such things. Much later, I studied about Chinese privilege, and I realized how prevalent it is in Singapore. Could my father have had a subconscious bias against Indians?

We didn't stop dating immediately. A few days later, Prateepan and I went to a nearby shopping mall, and when we were walking back, I got a call from my father. He asked me who I was with. I told him the truth because I don't like to lie to my parents. My father just ran out of the house to find us. But I was smart. Instead of walking back home directly, I called my mom and waited for her at the train station. That night was the first time I talked back to my father. I was crying. I was frustrated and stressed because I didn't understand what was happening. I didn't know how to handle the situation. So I told Prateepan that I couldn't continue this relationship. And soon, Prateepan left for Australia.

Prateepan: A common friend got us back together. He is Chinese but from Thailand. He went with me to study in Melbourne. All along, he would say things like you should message Carmen, you guys should reunite. Then when we came back to Singapore during our holidays, he invited me for dinner. And suddenly I saw Carmen at the dinner as well. Within a week from that night—on 2 January 2016—Carmen and I picked up from where we had left off. Even without this friend's help, we might have started again, but he did speed things up.

Carmen: It happened a year and a half after that incident with my father. We picked things up quickly. It all felt very natural. We really wanted to be together. I was really committed to him, so I prepared myself to talk to my father. Thankfully even before that, my mother had already discussed it with my father, and he was just fine with our relationship.

Prateepan: Carmen shares everything with her mother. On 5 January, she told her that she was seeing me again. Her mom said she would be more comfortable with me if I went to church every Sunday. Carmen and I had a big discussion. I had no objections. So I went to the church the very next day. I didn't have any intention of becoming a Christian. I just wanted to be there and perhaps learn more about Christianity which is Carmen's tradition.

Carmen: Religion plays a big part in my family, more than our Chinese culture. My father was even a pastor once. We went to church every Sunday. When I was a child, my mom brought me around for house visits to preach and convert. Once, we went to an Indian household, and I was so shocked and confused.

Why did they have so many idols of gods inside their house? In my world, we could only pray to one God. Why could Indians pray to more than one? Were they then supposed to choose one?

Prateepan: Two weeks later, Carmen's mother called me over to help fix their cupboard. Suddenly, her dad came in. Obviously, I was scared. But he said, 'Nice, nice to see you again. Okay. Okay. Carry on.'

I was like, okay, that was nice.

Ever since then, I have had zero conflicts with Carmen's dad. He has changed so drastically. Now he calls me over to have drinks with him. Every time we meet, it is just more bonding and more love.

Carmen: Now, my father wholly accepts Prateepan. I was worried that he might have issues with Prateepan being Hindu. But once, we were discussing our wedding, and I said Prateepan's family might want to have a Hindu wedding. Then my father said that is perfectly fine because he accepted that it is their culture.

Prateepan: We were indeed worried about that because my parents would definitely want a Hindu wedding, while her parents would definitely want a Christian-oriented one. I knew my parents would be okay as long as there was such a dual arrangement, but I wasn't sure about Carmen's side because they are staunch Christians. But then her father told me, 'I understand that you want to have a temple wedding, and it'd be nice to have it as well.'

Yet, for a long time, I felt some resistance from Carmen's mom. I couldn't figure out the reason. This continued until the dinner Carmen, her mother, and I had at Swensen's. Out of nowhere, Carmen's mom asked me to say the Sinner's prayer.

She then called my second sister, who had married a Christian and went to the same church as Carmen's family. She asked my sister to go through this prayer with me. I was so confused as I held the phone. What the hell was going on? Could somebody tell me? On the phone, my sister was laughing all along. My sister said, 'I don't know what's going on. I don't know what to say.' And then she just said something from some scripture, and it was just a sentence, and it happened so fast, and I repeated what she said. When it was all done, Carmen's mom said she felt very comfortable with me because now, I have been saved.

In Carmen's parents' eyes, I have become a Christian because I've said the Sinner's prayer. Ever since then, they haven't bothered me about being Christian. But I am still a Hindu. So, we got a little bit of figuring out to do on that note, yeah.

I became a part of their family very fast. Was race then really the issue? Maybe, our biggest hurdle was overcoming the religious differences in our background. After all, Carmen's family traditions are based more on Christianity than Chinese culture.

On the other hand, there was zero resistance from my family. My oldest sister was married to a Caucasian, and my second sister, to a Christian-Indian. So I had enough time to learn from my older siblings how and when to introduce a partner. I had seen their mistakes, like introducing a boyfriend too early and breaking up after that. I knew that if I brought someone home, it had to be the person I wanted to marry. That's why I didn't introduce Carmen to my family until 2018.

There is a running joke in my family about how my brother-in-law had to work so hard to earn my parent's acceptance while Carmen was welcomed in their first meeting itself, with the honour of being served food on a banana leaf. Well, this brother-in-law, the Christian-Indian, is himself to blame. He had piercings; he had a tattoo of my sister's name on his forearm;

he didn't want to study; he wasn't the traditional good boy. You know, when you meet your partner's parents in a complicated situation, you have to present yourself in a certain way. But he dug a hole for himself.

Honestly, the only reason why my parents have supported us so far is because of their assumption that while Carmen will stay Christian, I'm not going to become one. My mother will be devastated if I ever become a Christian. My family follows a lot of Hindu traditions. Especially when a child is born, he or she is taken to the temple, and many prayers and ceremonies follow. My brother-in-law, the Christian Indian, wasn't comfortable with that. When their child was born, they didn't take him to a temple for over two years. My mom had a heavy heart about that. She worried that something bad was going to happen to the child. There was also friction because they were raising the boy as a Christian, despite saying earlier that they would let him choose his own faith. My parents were already upset when my sister converted after her marriage.

Carmen: His family was very accommodating. It is really easy being with them. They always speak in English when I am around. We were watching this reality show in Tamil called *Big Boss* together, and his mother kept translating for me everything the actors said on the show. Once, his mother even apologized to me when she spoke in Tamil. I got confused and asked why she was apologizing. After some reflection, I realized that since I had the privilege of coming from the majority group in Singapore, I had never felt the need to apologize in similar situations. Unlike minorities, I never felt 'not included'.

Prateepan: When Carmen came into our family, she just got into it very quickly. She would scold me in front of my family. And when she is scolding me, my mom will start as well. That's the culture in my family.

Carmen: There are many differences between Prateepan and me, as well as between our respective families. No one in my family talks much. We can all be sitting around each other without saying anything. We don't talk while eating; we only eat. My parents won't ever tell me straight in my face if they disagree with my decisions. And then, maybe after a few years, when things pile up and there is a trigger point, they might bring it up all of a sudden. However, in Prateepan's family, there is always something to talk about. It's very awkward for them when no one is talking. So everyone will try to find something to chat about. Prateepan had to learn not to be uncomfortable with our family's silence. Many times, he becomes the one starting conversations at my house. Sometimes when Prateepan and I are quarrelling, he will get frustrated because I am not speaking, that I am not expressive enough. Whereas, funnily, sometimes I think he talks too much. Interestingly, this also makes me enjoy being with him and his family. At times, I wonder whether it was actually cultural or individual characteristic.

Prateepan: As for Carmen, I pick up her Singlish-ness when she speaks with her friends in that Chinese-orientated English. Carmen then becomes a different person altogether, sounding more aggressive. Sometimes she talks to me the same way. I will then say, 'Wait, why are you talking like that? Can you stop?'

Carmen: My mother said, 'Carmen, there's always something happening in an Indian family.' I have to learn how to fit into such an expressive culture. His family is always having parties. There's always something going on. There's always a reason to see everyone. Whenever his mom cooks something nice, everyone comes over to eat. If there is a wedding, there will be various events even before the wedding. Nowadays, since Prateepan is not here, for many of his family occasions, I go as his representative of sorts. Sometimes his mother asks me to pray to their gods or put the prayer ashes on my forehead, and I am fine with that. Instead of praying, I acknowledge the divine presence and thank them for their blessings. However, when I came back home, and I was still wearing those marks, my mom would ask me if I prayed, and I would say no. Because to me, I wouldn't consider what I did as praying. But I never felt like saying 'No,' to his mom. For me, it is all about accepting his culture and beliefs.

Prateepan: Carmen's family has a tradition of holding hands and praying before every meal, as many Christian families do. I felt awkward about this, even though the prayer is often about me. I had to adjust to it. Now I think it's nice that they bless each other.

I had to adjust to their family's food as well. It is blander. Carmen also exposed me to Chinese cuisine, and there are certain things that I still don't like, like bamboo shoots. But sometimes, when we are eating Indian food, Carmen would find it very salty while I wouldn't find it salty at all.

Carmen: Now, Indian food has become my comfort food. Every week, I go over to eat his mom's cooking. I am extremely grateful for that. At his house, I mostly eat with my hands, just like they do. His mother is very considerate and would offer me cutlery at times, but I find it so much easier to eat with my hands. Because their dishes have stronger flavours, I take more rice to blend them in, and fingers are much better for that.

Prateepan: There is this pressure of living up to what Carmen's dad would want me to be as a son-in-law, to be the man of the house. Maybe that's what their tradition is. But I come from a family where women dominate. Carmen's dad says, 'We are giving our daughter away to you.' I feel bad hearing this.

I am not taking away a daughter. It is something mutual, like a partnership. This idea of being the man of the house also puts an expectation of taking our future family down the path of Christianity. Her father doesn't really say that we need to raise our kids as Christians. But I can feel the unspoken pressure.

Carmen: So Prateepan and I are trying to create an environment within both families wherein they understand the need to be more accepting of each other. Now our families attend each other's festivals and celebrations. At Prateepan's sister's Indian wedding, my father really enjoyed himself, he even danced. That was the first time I saw my father dancing in my life, he is so uptight otherwise.

When we have children, we want them to be exposed to both religions and both cultures and let them pick what they feel most comfortable with. Regarding language, anyway, Prateepan doesn't really speak much Tamil. I can speak Chinese, but I cannot read and write. We haven't gone into specifics about raising our children because we haven't had much exposure to children yet. But we are learning from what's happening with our siblings.

Prateepan: As for our friends, they have always been very supportive of our relationship. But, there was this Chinese guy—Carmen's friend—who told her, 'Why are you going with this Indian guy? You can't find anyone else?'

Carmen: I don't remember that.

Prateepan: Sorry, I think my memory is stronger than Carmen's.

Carmen: That's true, he has a better memory when compared to me. But when I was studying at Polytechnique, and people didn't really see us together because Prateepan was away,

some friends would ask, 'Are you still together with him?'
It's like they assumed that we would have broken up already.
Maybe people did not acknowledge our kind of relationship as
something possible.

But I have never felt uncomfortable being together with
Prateepan in the streets. Prateepan, on the other hand, often
notices strangers staring at us. But I would always be oblivious
and wonder if it was because I had the privilege of being a
Chinese in Singapore.

Prateepan: In Singapore, people stare at us a lot, especially the
older Chinese. This happened if we went out for dinners or to
a mall. It annoyed me a lot. And Carmen was always oblivious
to all this. She's just looking straight all the time. But for me,
whenever people stare like this, I feel a little small. I don't know
why, but I can't help that feeling.

Nowadays, I just ignore it. Yet, this is why we don't hold
hands in public. I just don't want people to stare. I always have
this assumption, this belief that in the Singaporean context, an
Indian is less than a Chinese and that people will always stare
at me if they see me with a Chinese girl. Surprisingly, fewer
people stare at us when we are in India than in Singapore. We
were surprised.

Growing up, I was close to my Chinese neighbours and had
many Chinese friends. They were very close; we did everything
together. We would even have sleepovers. But I did face some
racially motivated incidents. When I was eight years old, my
close friend told me about this Chinese auntie who gave haircuts
for $2 only and then gifted a goldfish in a little bag. So we went
there, and she looked at me, and then she was like, 'No, go away.'
Why would she do that? This was my first experience of feeling
small. Another time was when we were at the playground. I was
holding on to another Chinese kid's bicycle. His mom came and

snatched away the bicycle. She said, 'Don't, don't, don't, don't steal the bicycle. Don't touch the bicycle.' But I wasn't doing anything with it. I was just holding it. And she was fine when other kids went cycling on it, but then those kids were Chinese. That, again made me feel small.

Then there is the number of times in my life I've heard this phrase, 'You're handsome for an Indian,' But what does it mean, 'for an Indian?' Why can't you just say handsome?

Carmen: Chinese privilege in Singapore is not very outright or obvious. It comes through in small ways that we don't even realize. Sometimes my mom would say that she didn't enjoy working with some Indian colleagues because they were too outspoken; she said that in a negative way. But my mother doesn't understand that we are more privileged in that we don't have to worry about many things in life, about not fitting in. Even in things like language, we often don't realize that we speak to each other in Chinese when Prateepan is around, knowing he can't understand what we are saying. That is not really right.

Prateepan: So when I got together with Carmen, I wondered whether I had to prove my worth to her family because I'm not Chinese. And honestly, I don't know where that stems from. Even after I was accepted into Carmen's family, there were times when I felt small as an Indian because of their unintentionally insensitive jokes. Once, her brother was talking about a Chinese guy who had become darker after National Service. So he said to me, 'Maybe that's your brother?' Carmen's brother found such a joke completely fine.

There was this incident in Singapore when a Chinese lecturer wearing a 'I love Singapore' T-shirt approached an interracial couple and told them that such relationships shouldn't happen. Carmen and I discussed it. What would we do if this happened to us? I said that I would just walk away. Carmen thinks I would have stood my ground.

We are very grateful that we didn't encounter such things ourselves. Otherwise, we would have found it hard to keep going. We already had a lot to go through—long distance, religious differences, and combining the two cultures. And then, if you throw that extra element of strangers abusing you, we would have lost all motivation.

So, whenever I felt small for being an Indian, I would stay away from my own culture. For instance, I wouldn't speak Tamil. But as I grew older, I learned that I needed to be who I am. I'm Indian. I need to embrace it.

In Singapore, it has gotten easier to be yourself as people have started talking more about Chinese privilege, that it actually exists.

I don't intend to come back to Singapore. So where will we be when I finish my studies? Where will we start our family? We need to plan all these things. So, we've discussed a lot about our future.

Carmen: There was this girl, my senior, who was in a similar situation. Her parents were completely against the idea of an Indian boyfriend then. She was asking me for advice, and then she disappeared. I think that they must have broken up. So, I want to send a message to interracial couples that it is important to remember that when it comes to love and relationships, the most important thing is to be true to yourself. As an advocate for interracial couples, I believe that your partner's race or ethnicity should not matter if you truly love and appreciate them for who they are. It's crucial to make your own decisions about whom you want to be with rather than conforming to someone else's expectations or prejudices.

Choosing a life partner is a deeply personal decision, and it's important to prioritize your own happiness and well-being in that process. If you allow others to influence your decisions, you may end up sacrificing your own happiness in the long run. So, my message to interracial couples is to trust your instincts and follow your heart, regardless of what anyone else thinks or says. By doing so, you can create a relationship built on a foundation of love, respect, and mutual understanding.

Prateepan: I advocate for interracial couples to stay together. Don't force it to happen, but if it does happen, don't be who you're not. Stay rooted in your culture because that's the beautiful thing about such relationships, merging two cultures into one. That is amazing. If I encounter a younger interracial couple who seem to be struggling with their relationship, I feel compelled to offer them my guidance and support. Through this act of kindness, I hope to send a powerful message to the older generation that true love knows no boundaries of race or religion. I believe that by supporting these couples, we can break down the barriers that have divided us for far too long. We can demonstrate to the world that love is a universal language that speaks to us all. It is a force that can overcome even the most deep-seated prejudices and biases.

That's the Kind of Damage
Families Can Cause

The story of Jack (name changed), thirties, Chinese–Malaysian, and Jill (name changed), thirties, Indian–Malaysian. They are married and live in Malaysia.

Jack: My father comes from a small town near Penang. It was a town of rubber tappers. Most of the residents there were Indians. I grew up as a Roman Catholic. At the church, almost everyone was Indian because, in Malaysia, the majority of Christians are Indians. So most of my friends there were Indians.

When I was in primary school, we moved to Kuala Lumpur. I studied in a private Mandarin school that was literally called China School. Everyone there was Chinese. After that, I joined a government school. Unfortunately, my father had a heart attack when I was in my late teens and that forced him to stop working. So I dropped out of school to work and support the family.

I had many girlfriends when in high school. Many of them were Chinese. We didn't have mobile phones then, so all of us siblings would fight for the phone to talk to our respective partners. Then our parents would look at the phone bill and ask each one of us, 'Whose number is this? And who is this one?'

Jill: My father comes from Negeri Sembilan, and my mother is from Pahang. They got married without their parents' approval.

My father was a Roman Catholic, and my mother was a high-caste Hindu. My father was in the military and then worked as an aircraft technician. Because of his job, we moved around Malaysia a lot. So my childhood was all about changing schools. I studied in five primary schools and three high schools. So it was hard to make real friends. I spent most of my time reading because books were the only constant in my life. I have always been an extreme introvert. Even now, Jack and our baby are the only people allowed inside my bubble. I could not speak Tamil even though our parents talked to each other in Tamil. All of us siblings can understand Tamil, but we could never speak it. Being an introvert, having to change so many schools, and not being able to speak Tamil, I got picked on a lot, especially by people from my own community—the Tamils. My teachers also bullied me. So childhood was not much fun.

I started work after high school at the age of eighteen. My parents hadn't planned well about our further education, so I took things into my own hands and began working.

When I was a child, my parents converted to Protestantism. Such converts are more fanatical about their newfound faith. So, anything related to Indian culture became taboo. It was always our religion first. It was always the Bible. Since our own Indian culture was so suppressed at home, I got early exposure to other cultures. Malaysia is amazing that way. To get exposure to other cultures, you just have to switch on the TV or open your door.

In any case, I was more interested in non-Indian people and cultures. This was not only because I was curious but also because, from a very young age, I equated Indian culture to whatever negative I saw around me: domestic violence, poor status of women, racism, and intolerance. The Chinese and the Malay people were more accepting of me. So I didn't want anything to do with anything Indian.

Also, later my mother started going back to her family. So she would now ask us to go to the temples. All along, you told us these beliefs were wrong, and now you are asking us to go back to them. We were all so confused. From Roman Catholic to Protestant to Hindu—what was happening?

Jack: People in my family got married outside our races. My eldest sister married a Pakistani, my second sister married a Malay. This is how Malaysia is. So my parents were more open even though not the most open. My parents can be hot-headed, and they are not politically correct; they speak without any filter. So they would make jokes about other races, some tasteful, some not. My mother wanted me to marry someone Chinese, just because of the cultural similarities.

Regarding my eldest sister, my parents were initially concerned because of the differences in religion, as her husband was a Muslim. But my father eventually told my sister, 'If you are going to become a Muslim, just be a good Muslim. If you're going to be his wife, be a good wife.'

As for me, I was always attracted to Indian culture. The main reason for this is Indian food. I just love the curries and the flavours. My wife says Indian food has just one flavour—spicy, but it is not so. I always want to eat Indian food, like in a banana leaf, with good, nice, and thick curry, not some watered-down version.

Jill: Jack eats how an Indian man eats, with his hands. He can even eat yoghurt with his hands. He knows his food. And there I will be asking for a fork and spoon for myself.

Jack: My earlier relationships with Chinese girls didn't work out. There's something about the Chinese culture in Malaysia, it is very money focused. We are always thinking of a person as does he earn enough, have a good education, and stay in the best area in town. You must study business, medicine, law, or computer. I didn't like that part. So it was hard when I was dating Chinese girls. In the China School I studied in, there were many rich brats. They got what they wanted. They had big pocket money. I had very little allowance. They came in fancy cars. I came on a school bus. When you are dating, the girl expects the boy to be the one providing all the time. My boyfriend must have a car, my boyfriend must take me to nice restaurants and get me expensive handbags.

On the other hand, Indian girls were much less materialistic. Unfortunately, the stereotypes in Malaysia about Indian women—that they are brought up to serve their men—turned out to be true for me. My Indian girlfriends from the past would look to me for the simplest of decisions. Where do you want to eat? She would say, 'Up to you.' What do you want to eat? 'Anything you want.' I would later find out that even though they didn't actually like my choice, they just followed me. I didn't want that kind of relationship. It became boring. A relationship has to be a two-way street. There has to be both giving and taking. I want to be able to communicate. That is why I love my wife because she wasn't one that took instruction.

Jill: As for me, Chinese culture made more sense in my head rather than Indian culture because Indian culture is so saturated with religion. I love their Mid-Autumn Festival and the Lunar New Year. I love the myths and the stories associated with them. I used to watch Mandarin and Cantonese shows.

Anyway, I was never approached by Indian men. I don't know why. Maybe because I don't speak the language. Maybe it's just me. It's the same with my sister, who is seven years younger.

I told my parents, 'Absolutely no matchmaking for me.' That's a big deal for Indians. When you grow up in a household where the head of the family is so narcissistic, that person has already made the check boxes for his daughter's husband—that he's Indian, that he needs to be like him. Matchmaking is about balance of power—older people dominating their children. But when you make wrong decisions, people suffer for life.

I saw some disastrous results from matchmaking. My father did matchmaking for my friend, who got married into a family of narcissistic people. It was disastrous. And she would tell me, 'Your father arranged for this.' So I told my parents, 'No, arranged marriage is not happening for me.' I grew up in an environment of domestic abuse. It was not easy seeing my mother getting beaten, being helpless. It was not easy seeing how a man treats a woman with that Indian mindset, a mindset that does not want to evolve and be better. I wanted a partner who understood that a woman is not his punching bag. And the only way I could think about that was to move away from the Indian culture. So I told my parents, 'I would die alone rather than have you matchmaking for me.' And my dad took it very badly.

So when I went out to the world, to work at the age of eighteen, I was not looking for a partner. I was just getting out of a troubled house. I was just trying to make sense of my life. Then somebody 'upstairs' loved me enough to give me Jack. And I married the first man I dated.

We were in the same company. He was my boss. I was just starting out, and when I went for a team meeting, and there walks in this cocky Chinese guy in red. He was unbearable. He was so arrogant. He was bullying me.

Jack: I didn't bully her. She was just lazy [laughs]. To be fair, she was only eighteen years old. So, she didn't have the work ethic yet. I was a strict manager. I always believed that my staff should do their own homework before seeking guidance. I wanted them to be independent. That's how I wanted to bring up my team members. And they always got promoted. She hated me back then, but she also got promoted.

Jill: He was known as General Chin. But General Chin was genuine. I respected his unique way of dealing with people. It was interesting to watch him at work. Slowly we got into a relationship. It took a long time. Because I found it hard to trust anyone. But he was so kind. Once, I was very sick and he brought me a healing tea made by his mother. It was a special tea. I was so surprised. I saw somebody caring for another without expecting any benefits. That kindness is still there. And it still astounds me. I've not had the easiest life, and I felt very lucky to actually find a man who understands me despite all the cultural differences.

Jack: I admit I am guilty of totally abusing my status as a boss. I took her number. I messaged and called her all the time. I was most attracted to her intelligence. And she was not a stereotypical Indian lady who would say, 'My dream is to travel the world.' When we interviewed her for our call centre and asked about her ambition, she said, 'I want to be an aeronautical engineer.' I know no one in their right mind grows up wanting to work in a call centre. So Jill was so real. She was not at all materialistic. She was curious. She wanted to know more. In her, I found another nerd like myself.

Jill: My parents were not happy when I told them about Jack. This was because he was not an Indian. They were also not happy that Jack's sisters had converted to Islam after they got married. But was I marrying his sisters?

Jack: But I was very persistent. I had to prove to them that I could take care of their daughter. Once they saw that I spoke a bit of Tamil, they lightened up a bit. But unfortunately, till the very end of their days, they never accepted me. Jill's siblings largely accepted me, but her parents were not comfortable with me till the day they passed away.

It was not just because I am not an Indian. I also came from a religion her father had converted out of. Jill's mom told her that people like me tend to cheat on women, and that we do not treat women right. Her father had other intentions—he preferred another Indian guy. Jill may not agree with this, but her father dropped me a lot of hints about this. Every time there was a family function that I was invited to, magically, this guy was also there.

Jill: We dated for eight years before we got married. It was very difficult. But by then, I was twenty-six, and my dad felt he had no choice but to agree. Because in his head, he was probably thinking, 'Oh my god, my daughter is twenty-six, and she's not married.' I stayed strong. I was adamant about getting married on my terms. There is something about growing up watching your mother getting beaten, you either become a weaker woman, or it makes you stronger. I became stronger. I'd rather be happy alone than married and unhappy. So when I got to twenty-six, my parents were so scared that I would just run away. So my dad reluctantly said, 'Yes.'

Even then, it was not easy. They tried to create as much hassle as they could. We wanted to get married on a specific date, our eighth anniversary of being together, which was also Valentine's Day in the Chinese calendar. My family didn't like this. They were like, 'How can you do this? Why is it so rushed? Why this, why that? Are you pregnant?'

Those three months running up to our wedding were very stressful. You're supposed to be happy, you're supposed to be excited. But no, I had to deal with all this stress. They were trying to convince me I was pregnant. I begged my father not to make a big deal out of it. What I wanted was very simple—registration followed by a family dinner. But now they wanted a big event. They were more concerned about what other people would be saying about us. That's the cultural side of Indians in Malaysia. It is very important what other people will say. And their weddings are supposed to be big events. But I didn't want all that.

Jack: Her father told me, 'If you want to marry my daughter, you must "declare" that you married my daughter. Because I'm not going to let my daughter live with you because you just registered. There has to be a proper, big event.' I didn't really understand what was happening. Her father's side actually wanted to do Hindu-style celebrations while they were Christians. It was all very confusing.

 Then one day, he called me to inform me that there was a ceremony that my future bride had to attend, but I couldn't because the men were not allowed. They will put Jill up on stage, literally wearing just lingerie, and then cover her in milk and turmeric. I said no way is my wife going to be shown in public like that. This became a huge argument. They said that I was letting logic get in the way of tradition. I said, 'How can you not let logic get in the way of tradition?'

Jill: There was so much manipulation going on. I said no to many such ceremonies. Because I didn't identify with them. But they would then go behind my back and argue with Jack. There was another occasion when I had to go and give the invitation card. Even such a simple thing became difficult. In modern times, a wedding invitation is just a PDF file. In the last ten years, my friends and cousins who got married would just WhatsApp or email me. But in my case, they wanted a proper physical card and a ceremony associated with that— the card is put on a platter with fruits and other things, and many people are invited. When I was going to give the card to my father's mother—I will not call her my grandmother but my father's mother—she looked at me and said publicly, 'Why are you going through all this trouble? Yours is not a real marriage anyway.' When I gave it to my friends and relatives, they all laughed, 'What age are you living in?' But there's only so much I could fight against, only so much I could say no to. So I just lost certain battles to marry the man I loved.

Jack: Her father even hijacked the wedding dinner. My mom can't eat spicy food because of some medical condition. Earlier, Jill's father said that he would be hiring some caterers to test the dishes. But it never happened. He said that only to pacify me. He had already made all the arrangements, having more Indian-centric food rather than making it a balance. But we had Chinese guests too. When we brought this up, he even said, 'I gave you Chinese food already, no? The vegetables?'

Jill: As a bride, I was unhappy with everything—from my hair to my clothes to everything else. My father arranged everything. He was worried about losing face. It didn't matter what the bride or the groom wanted. For him, it was like, 'I already gave you a choice to marry who you wanted to.' So I had to keep thinking about what was important—the man I loved.

Jack: It was very tricky. My mom, being a mother, knows who she brought up. She knows I'm not a very accommodating guy and that I can be firm with my opinions and can get impatient when things don't make sense. So she asked me, 'Are you okay or not? Because you are giving in a lot.' But I told her that nothing changes the fact that I loved Jill. My family understood that we needed to be more tolerant since Jill's side was being so difficult. So we could not invite many people from our family, Jill's side had already taken up 80 per cent of the attendance list.

Jill: On the other hand, I couldn't have asked for better in-laws. It was not lost on me that in a Chinese family, marrying the only son is a big deal. So I was very afraid of how I would handle this. But his side treated me with nothing but love. His father's younger sister—the first person in the family I got introduced to—was nothing but welcoming to me. As I talked more to my mother-in-law and got to know each other, I could sense that she doesn't feel the loss of not having a Chinese daughter-in-law. I love her tremendously, and she has been nothing but the best mother-in-law.

Jack: There were some issues about religion. My godmother made some snarky comments like it was not a real marriage under the eyes of God because we didn't get married in a church. I don't take such comments lightly, so I faced her squarely. She stopped. The beautiful part about it is that she didn't take it badly. She now treats Jill like her god-daughter.

My mother is in love with Jill. Both my parents message her, 'How are you, my daughter?' None of them message me. The only time they message me, it reads like, 'Our toilet broke. Can you come this weekend to fix it?' or 'Our car has broken down. Can you come?'

When it comes to outsiders responding to us, Malaysia can be interesting. We can be very racist in public but very accepting in private. So when we go out together, people tend to stare. Unfortunately, many still think my wife is my maid because she takes care of the baby.

Jill: People in my housing area think he's a single dad. No one asks me, but they ask his sister, who lives a few doors down.

Sometimes they think the sister is the maid because she is darker than Jack.

Jack: So people think I have a lot of maids. They think I can't afford anything else because that's the only way I like to spend money, having maids.

Indian men will stare at her to show that they are disappointed with her, and then they stare at me, 'Why did I steal one of them?' So we get a lot of such looks. The only place where we don't feel judged is Penang. There the looks I get from Indian men suggest, 'Hey, nice. Yeah?' And then the Chinese will look at Jill, suggesting, 'Very nice. Yeah?' It is obvious from the way they smile sideways. Because Penang is different from the rest of Malaysia. In Penang, you can see a Chinese man and a Malay man and an Indian man sitting and having coffee together. You see Indians speaking Malay and Malays speaking Chinese. So when we go to Penang, we feel so accepted. That's what Malaysia is supposed to be.

Jill: So I dread going to Indian-run outlets like banana leaf restaurants. I am always judged because I can't speak Tamil, and I am with him who can. Once, we went to this Indian restaurant, and the Tamil waiter said something insulting to me because Jack could order in Tamil while I couldn't. This was a new level of racism I was facing. The guy said, 'Even this innocent Chinese fellow can get water in Tamil, and you, an Indian, can't?'

But now, I can't be bothered any more. If someone is uncomfortable in my presence, I just walk away. If you are not paying my bills, if you are not living in my home, then your opinion doesn't count. I will never be happy if I take everyone's opinion into account.

Jack: In Malaysia, Indians are very close-knit. They are more stringent with their culture. They want Indians to marry Indians only. The Chinese are somewhat similar. Because the Chinese here are fed up with what people say about us, because we eat pork, or our pagan beliefs like Buddhism and Taoism. Also, the Chinese are richer. So the Chinese generally tend to marry within the race.

Jill: There is a pecking order for interracial marriage: first white, then Chinese, then Indian, then African or Black. The colour of the skin plays a huge role. You will especially see Indians with fairer skin biased against Indians with darker skin. I don't know why we react like that. And there is this whole issue of other races marrying Malays because of the religious conversion law.

When people see a mixed baby like our daughter, they just don't know how to process it. So their first reaction when they see our child is, 'She doesn't look like you at all.'

Oh my god.

Jack: These kinds of comments are not offensive at first, but after you hear it for the fortieth and fiftieth time, you wonder, what are they trying to say?

Jill: I had a very stressful pregnancy. January 2019, I found out that I was pregnant. April 2019, my mother died then August 2019, my father died, and then two weeks later, our baby was born. Just like our wedding was difficult, having two funerals with conflicting people was also difficult. Then, the delivery was complicated. We almost lost her. So I'm just happy with however she is, whatever she looks like, as long as she's healthy. But people want to judge immediately when they see her.

So we will tell our daughter that Mummy and Daddy are here for you. You don't have to be afraid to talk to us. Because that's what I couldn't do with my own parents. Our wedding was so stressful for me. By the end of that year, my body just gave up. I fell sick, and I developed this chronic auto-immune disease. From all that stress, my body just said that it was done. That's the kind of damage families can cause. So with our daughter, I will tell her that there's nothing that we can't solve together.

What I want to impart to her is that culture does not make a person. You make your own choices. You choose what you feel is right. So you should have a true heart, free from judging people because of what they were born into. Nobody had a choice in that. I also want her to learn how to deal with being judged because the world will still judge. Then, we would have done half our job as parents.

And then sometimes the universe will work itself out if your heart is right. A small example is the fact that our daughter was born on Valentine's Day in the Lunar Calendar, the same day we got married. We didn't plan it. It just happened.

It Was Like Bollywood

Story of Josephine, thirties, Chinese–American from India, and Abhishek Jaiswal, thirties, Indian–American from India. They are married. They live in the United States of America.

Josephine: I come from the Chinese community in India. My grandfather came from China to Calcutta in the 1930s. My parents were born and raised in Kolkata but then migrated to Hyderabad. Like any other Chinese family in India, my father was a chef, and my mother worked in a beauty salon. I have two older brothers. The eldest is eleven years older than me. My family was Buddhist but converted to Catholicism before I was born.

My family was very traditional and conservative. It was very difficult for me to make them accept my relationship with someone who was not Chinese. I was beaten up, locked in my room, and followed around. It was like Bollywood.

Abhishek: I was born and brought up in Hyderabad, India. I come from a family with a business background. I was a very shy and timid guy in school but opened up during my high school days.

Josephine: I was born in Hyderabad too. The Chinese community there—with about fifty families—is much smaller than the one in Kolkata, which probably has over 500 left. But my parents retained a strong connection with the Kolkata Chinese. We often visited Kolkata and stayed at our aunt's house.

At home, my parents followed many Chinese traditions, like the Chinese New Year and the Moon Festival. They made sure of our participation in these. But there was a lot of Indian influence as well. My mother would take us to Hindu temples, even after they had converted to Christianity. We spoke Hakka at home, but Hindi when outside.

My parents were not well educated. Their life was limited to their work and raising three kids. They were not aware of much beyond that. Perhaps that is why they never talked about the political tensions between India and China or how the Chinese in India were interned in Rajasthan after the 1962 war because of suspicion.[8]

At school, I stood out among the other kids. Not just because I was Chinese, but also because I was involved in many extra-curricular activities. Everyone knew me at school. I had many good friends, not just from my class but also from those above and below. In college, I did a lot of organizing, and a lot of volunteering, with UNICEF etc. I was also with the National Cadet Corps (NCC) Air Wing.

As a Chinese person, I never faced any discrimination. The teachers treated us all the same. They actually favoured me a little. Maybe, because I was good at sports. I represented Hyderabad in mountaineering. My teachers were very encouraging. My parents were too.

And then I met Abhishek, on the eve of Y2K.

---

[8] After the 1962 war, India passed the Defence of India Act under which many Chinese-origin persons living in India were detained.

Abhishek: I was a very good friend of Josephine's second brother. On Y2K eve, we both wanted to go to this New Year's Party. But they didn't allow any stags. So her brother came up with this brilliant idea to bring Josephine and her friend along.

At the party, Josephine and I ended up dancing together. That is how we met.

Josephine: We started just as friends. There was no dating. We kept in touch through email. And one day, all of a sudden, he said, 'Would you like to meet?' Then one thing led to another.

What really brought us close was my cousin's attempt to marry me. Well, this is common among the Chinese community in India. It is so small and so closed that most marriages are a mix of arranged and love. My eldest brother's wife is also a distant cousin, someone my grandfather had liked since she was a child.

But I was just not into this cousin. I was only seventeen then, in my first year of college. So I told him that I already liked Abhishek. Abhishek wasn't even my boyfriend then. We only hung out for coffee sometimes, just like teenagers do. But I just wanted to get rid of my cousin. And then this cousin blurted everything out to my parents. My family went crazy.

All hell broke loose. My two older brothers behaved like typical elder brothers, the type you see in films. From that point onwards, my eldest brother stood next to me whenever I got a call on my bulky Nokia phone. Who am I talking to? What am I saying? He checked all my messages and my call list. My family beat me up many times. Sometimes, they locked me up. Then they barred me from going out alone. My dad or my brother, or my mom, would go with me, even if I just needed to get something from a neighbourhood shop. When I went for my multimedia classes, my eldest brother used to just storm inside the class to check if I was there. I was miserable.

I told Abhishek about this. He assured me and supported me. What actually got us closer was the contrast of this comfort and support I got from Abhishek as opposed to how my own family went against me. That is how we ended up as a couple.

Abhishek: Her second brother—my good friend—called me and asked me to stay away from Josephine. After that, he stopped talking to me for seven or eight years.

Josephine: My family's anger was only because Abhishek is from a different culture, because he was Indian. I don't think it was about skin colour or any fear that Indian men would be more dominant in the relationship. All the young Chinese women in India are well-educated. They can stand up for themselves whether they are married to an Indian or Chinese. My family was not into my cousin either. My mom had told his mother that we couldn't get married because we were so closely related. It was just about Abhishek coming from a different race.

People from the Chinese community in India don't want any mixing—only Chinese with Chinese. Maybe because this community in India is so small, they want to preserve it. Perhaps social pressure is another factor. What will other Chinese people say? Everybody in the Chinese community knows who is staying where, how many children they have, and what they are doing—it is easy to pinpoint everyone. My brother told me that I was like the princess of the family, the family's pride, and that I had never done things that would make my parents bow their heads in shame. I came in the newspapers. I did short films and mountaineering. I have never heard of any other Chinese boy or girl doing it. My brothers never did it. I was the first one in my family to get a higher education. Eventually, I came to the US to do my master's and then became an American citizen. Because of all these, I was like a star of the community. And then I tell them that I want to marry outside my race? That's why they went crazy. They tried all that emotional blackmailing—now you've become too big, you've outgrown this house, you've achieved so much that you're not going to listen to us any more. What will other the Chinese people say?

But I said that I don't care what others say. All that matters is that the boy and I are compatible and love each other. Other people will not give us any money and raise my family, right? But according to my family, my life would be wasted if I married outside. They tried many times to make me talk to Chinese boys. When I met them, I would bluntly say, 'I'm only talking to you because my mom and dad asked me to. Don't even think that anything will happen.'

Abhishek: Given the complexity, we thought that the only way for us to move forward was to escape India and get ourselves established somewhere else and then ultimately convince our parents to accept our relationship. That was the plan. We thought this was a better approach than eloping. We didn't want to go against our parents' wishes. We were not raised like that. We wanted to stay within our cultural norms.

Josephine: We were good kids. I could have just walked away from my family. We could've just gotten married in the US, and nobody would know about it. But I believe that in a marriage, parents from both sides should agree and bless the couple so that they have a happy married life.

Since my family wouldn't let me talk to Abhishek on the phone, email and internet chat were the only way we could stay in touch (they couldn't catch me this way because my mom was uneducated and my brother came home late). Over this, we made this plan of both going to the US.

My application to the university in the US got accepted first. My second brother was already in New York then. So I stayed with him at first because my university was also in New York. But once there, my brother took away my passport and state ID. My family feared that I would just run away. So my brother became like a security guard, keeping an eye on me at all times.

I didn't like what was happening. I am a very independent person. So I looked for another school, and then I moved to California. I applied for Abhishek at the same university. In the form, I put him as my brother because I couldn't say he was a boyfriend. But then the university called my actual brother to clarify something—I didn't have a phone and had put his number in the form as I didn't expect the university to call. My brother flipped. So I got caught once more, and the whole drama started again.

A month later, Abhishek came over to the US and joined the college. We began living together. My family would ask me, 'Are you still in touch with him?' I would say, 'No.' I told them that Abhishek's visa had got rejected. If my brother came to visit me, Abhishek would take all his luggage and move out to another friend's. So we had to do a lot of juggling. This went on for five years, from 2008 to 2013. The first thing on our agenda was to complete our studies so that we were on our feet. We hoped that after all that was done and we both began working, my family would eventually accept our relationship.

I got a job in the US Army, and then in 2012, I told my family that I wanted to marry Abhishek. My mom said, 'You said you were not going to be in touch with him, and now you're back with him.' My eldest brother tried to blackmail me, 'Because of you, mom is crying. She's not able to sleep. And when father sees her crying, he starts crying too.'

Abhishek: We supported each other all this long. Many times, either of us would hit a low and think of separating because it was all so tough. But then the other person would say that these dark clouds should pass, that we must stay strong. Let's not give up. Let's fight it through. Somehow, we would just get back to each other again.

Josephine: I was the more persistent one.

Abhishek: Yes, she was.

Josephine: I was thick-skinned and determined. If I decided I wanted this, I would want this. Yet, it was important for us to get our parent's consent.

Eventually, my parents gave in. My second brother also accepted. But my eldest brother was still against it. My parents would meet Abhishek a few times, and they would give us the go-ahead. But then, when they met my eldest brother again, it would be back to square one. My brother is very conservative, maybe because he spent so much time with my grandfather when growing up. He would say, 'Our Chinese culture should remain.'

My parents said I needed to convince my brother. But why? He got to choose his own partner. But when it comes to me, why cannot I marry who I want to? How is that fair? At that time, my brother's eldest daughter was eleven or twelve. So my brother told me, 'If you are going to marry him, I'm going to marry my daughter off at eighteen.' I said, 'You can get her married at whatever age you feel is right for her. Don't say that it is because of me.' The girl is now twenty-five years old and still not married.

Abhishek: My parents didn't react as adversely as her parents did. They said, 'Okay, if he likes her and is happy, then we know they're going to be happy together.' Josephine's brother— my good friend—used to come home often. So my parents had a good impression of their family. They thought of them as very hardworking. My mom had also met Josephine a couple of times and thought of her as a good girl with good values. But my dad was a little hesitant because Josephine was a Catholic Christian. He asked me, 'Will you convert? Will you forget Hinduism?' He was relieved when I said I had no such plans. My mom also helped to convince him.

Josephine: I don't know what it is with the boy's side—they always find it easier to convince the parents. It's always the girl's side that has problems in such cases. Maybe because I had older brothers. I wish I had an older sister; I'm pretty sure she would have a softer heart. But it is so much harder to deal with older brothers. My eldest brother was the most against us. But even the second brother teamed up with them, even though he was Abhishek's good friend.

Abhishek: But around 2012, her second brother started talking to me again. He even welcomed me to his house in New York.

Josephine: So, we eventually got married in 2013. Well, in 2010, we secretly had a court wedding. I didn't tell this to anyone. That was the first of the five weddings we ended up having. That wedding was required for us to file Abhishek's citizenship application for the US. Once our families were all fine, we told them that we were coming to India to get married but that, for various reasons, we needed to get married in the US before that. The real purpose was to ensure everything was done and dusted before anyone did any new drama once we went to India. So, in 2013, we first had a renewal of vows in the US. Then in India, we had our third wedding, which was an Indian-style wedding and then the fourth, which was a small tea ceremony, and then the fifth and final, the one in the church. My family wasn't very cooperative during all this, but it got done.

We have been married for ten years now. We have three kids.

Abhishek: Things have been simpler since then. We are now one big family—a set of twins and an elder daughter. And we are all together.

Josephine: His parents have very willingly accepted me and are very nice to me. His mom is the humblest person I've ever seen. They stayed with us during my pregnancies. My second set was twins, and I was in bed for three months. They took care of my oldest daughter during that time. It would have been very hard without their support.

As for my family, my parents never said anything directly to Abhishek anyway. From the bottom of their hearts, they knew that Abhishek was a good boy and would be a good partner. Their earlier resistance was perhaps because of my eldest brother's influence.

I still feel the difference from my eldest brother and his family. My mom died in 2016. She was diagnosed with breast cancer in 2012 and then with leukemia. My eldest brother sort of blames me for all that. Now that our mother is gone, I think our eldest brother should be the bridge between all the siblings. He should be the one trying to bring the family closer together. He does that in talking, but I don't see that in his actions.

Abhishek: As for outsiders, we haven't faced any issues from them. My friends have always been very supportive. Earlier, some would say, 'Why are you dating your friend's sister? Why would you do that? Why would you betray your friend?' But that was it.

Over here in the US, the neighbourhood we live in is relatively well-off and fairly mixed. So we don't face any challenges. Our kids have many friends. They get invited for sleepovers all the time.

Josephine: We do get some looks sometimes when we go out together, but that's about it. During Covid, there was a lot of anti-Chinese sentiment in the US. But we didn't face anything in Virginia. My brother, who lives in New York, says that he has experienced discrimination and hostility first-hand. We also didn't face anything during those times because we were always at home—both of us worked from home, and the kids were always at home.

Abhishek: Between us, our cultural differences haven't mattered much. Josephine is very open-minded and has never mentioned anything about conversion to Christianity. Actually, she is more of a Hindu than I am. I am much less religious.

Josephine: There's just one superpower, and all gods are equal. I go to temples, I go to churches, I go to mosques. I didn't believe in a lot of Catholic preaching myself, and I was always very interested in learning Hindu mythologies. As a child, I eagerly waited for Sundays when they showed *Ramayana* on TV. So, my husband is fine, and I'm fine.

Regarding food matters, I like Chinese food, but I cook more Indian food because I was born and raised there. Growing up, I ate a lot more Indian food than Chinese.

We mostly speak in English with the kids. But my husband and I speak both Hindi and English to each other.

I cannot think that I am not Chinese, but I'm more of an Indian as well. I especially miss my childhood in India—those college days and the friends I had back then. Those days are the best memories I have. That is why I joined the Facebook group 'Hakka from India,' because I wanted to keep my roots.

I do want our kids to know the Chinese traditions I learned from my mom when I grew up. I'm Chinese, so they're half-Chinese. They need to know they are. During Chinese New Year, I do the same things as my mother did. But, we celebrate things from Indian culture too, like Diwali and other festivals. We go to the temple as a family.

It has been such a long journey for us. We have been with each other through thick and thin. I have always wanted to write a book about it. Knock on wood, we are still happily married. We have three happy kids. That's all that matters.

III

When unfamiliar with a different race, we often rely on social media and the internet to shape our perceptions. In these cases, an interracial marriage becomes more about marrying an 'Indian' or a 'Chinese' rather than a specific person. The lack of first-hand experience leads to assumptions and biases.

Interestingly, after entering into such a marriage, one may form a new perception of the other race through 'new' first-hand experiences. This journey also prompts the individuals involved to redefine their own racial identity and evaluate how connected they should remain to their respective cultures. Many individuals in these relationships find themselves mourning a loss of connection to their own culture and worry about their children's identity and the adjustments they'll have to make.

For some, these concerns may feel effortless to navigate, but for others, unspoken thoughts keep lingering: Have I betrayed my own culture? What price am I paying by marrying outside of it? In societies like Australia where cosmopolitanism has become the 'norm', do these concerns become irrelevant? Do Indians and Chinese naturally gravitate towards each other in such societies due to fundamental similarities in their value systems? Is it, then, possible to form new, syncretic identities?

We Get Left Out of Many Social Occasions

Story of Amit (name changed), thirties, Indian–Singaporean from India, and Audrey (name changed), thirties, Chinese–Singaporean from China. They are married and live in Singapore.

Amit: I come from a typical lower-middle-income Indian family. My father had a government job, and he moved around a lot. We moved with him, but it was always within tier-three towns in India. The family value was centred around studying hard. I followed the typical middle-income career path in India, studying engineering and then working as a software engineer, never having a girlfriend all this while.

I met Audrey in 2010, and we got married in 2015. A lot happened within those five years, from getting estranged from my family to just ensuring that we, too, were comfortable with each other. It was an emotionally difficult journey.

Audrey: I, too, grew up in a tier-three city, in north-east China. As a child, I witnessed my parents having a difficult relationship. At home, it was always fight on, fight off, fight on, fight off, between the two. My father was always drinking. It was not easy for us. My grandfather was the one who cared for me. I was really close to him.

Growing up, we focused on studying hard and getting into a top university. I got into one, in a city forty-four hours away from home by train. That was part of the reason I just didn't want to come back home that often. In my fourth year at the university, I got an opportunity to study in Singapore. There, I met Amit. He was studying part-time in the same course as me. I only saw him attending the first few lessons. He didn't show up after that.

We connected again after I graduated. I was trying to find a job in Singapore and so reached out blindly to all such part-time classmates—who were already working—if they knew of any openings in their company. Amit referred me to one. Eventually, I got a job, but not through his referral. Yet, we started going out together, and here we are today.

Amit: Audrey and I met a couple of times after I helped her get that interview. At that time, I was sharing an apartment with two other guys. Naturally, we talked a lot about girls. One day, we were drinking together, and I talked to them about Audrey and how nice she was. They egged me on to write to her, so I shot an email—an expression of interest—saying we had become more than friends.

Audrey: I didn't even reply to that email.

Amit: That email went in August 2010, and by December of that year, we had begun dating.

Audrey: My mother only came to know about us in 2012. I had gone back home on vacation, and once there, my mother asked me to pray to get a suitable partner. I said that I won't because I had already met someone, and he was not Chinese but Indian. Initially, she didn't react much. But then, she must have done some research about India. In Chinese media, many things about India are not nice—there are only reports of rapes, how some men have over twenty wives, and how India is poor and dirty. She became worried that in India, women don't go out to work, they are made to take care of children, and the place is very religious. Soon, she got very opposed to the idea of us getting together.

Amit: So my main enemy was Google or Baidu. Because of this, Audrey's mother made me agree to never settle down in India for good.

Audrey: Maybe she contrasted India with Japan because my mother worked as an interpreter for Japanese and had also visited Japan. She would always talk about how clean Japan is—you can sit down on the street, and your dress doesn't even get dirty. So she always encouraged me to go to places more developed than China.

I tried hard to convince her. I became a salesman—for Amit and for India. I just kept saying good things about him to my mother—that he's so smart, and so kind, caring, that he is an upright person, and that he's physically active. He dragged me to run (exercise). I told her that the divorce rate in India is very low.

Amit: Well, if one wants to convince the parents, he or she must tell them good things about the other person.

Audrey: But I didn't lie one bit. It was just how I saw him. In 2013, Amit met my mother. Over time, she agreed to the relationship.

As for my father, he and my mother divorced when I was in my third year of university. My father didn't want me to come to Singapore. But my mother supported me then. As such, my relationship with him wasn't very good. So, he didn't say anything directly to me. But when my mother first told him about Amit, he said, 'If it were not for you, then she would never be marrying an Indian.' My mother had no words to respond to such an accusation.

Amit: So, there was a big difference between Audrey and me, in where we were in our respective stories. Audrey told her mom about us only sometime in 2012. But by early 2011, I had already fought with my parents. I was in the Second World War while Audrey was still in the first.

It was far more intense on my side. India has so many more layers of complexity—there is religion, there is caste, and then there is sub-caste. Your parents want to ensure you are married within as fine a sub-group as a sub-sub-caste. All this is so ingrained in our belief system that no one could ever imagine me marrying a non-Indian. It didn't even cross my own mind. I was always ready for an arranged marriage. I thought that was the best way to go. Anyway, I was never popular with girls, and I never made any special effort to reach out to girls. My mindset became more open only after I came to Singapore.

As I sensed our relationship getting more serious, I began dropping hints to my parents. They got the hint and asked me to come home under some pretext. Once I went, they arranged for me to meet a girl they liked, who lived just half a kilometre away. My dad was so invested in this arrangement; he must have imagined her as the future daughter-in-law all along. So that was my parent's strategy to deal with my hints about Audrey. But I knew well what was going on in their mind.

It was a traumatic week. Upon arriving, I told my mom about my situation in no uncertain terms. In one go, I dropped too many bombshells—that there was a girl already, that she was Chinese, and that she was called Audrey (her Chinese name is absolutely unfamiliar to Indians). My mom is an emotional person. She cried a lot.

I still met the girl whose family they had made an arrangement with. I told her she was nice, but nothing would happen between us. My mother still kept saying, 'Let's see. You will eventually fall in love with this girl we have arranged.' But I was very clear in my mind about Audrey. Call it stupid love or young love, but I had this mindset that come whatever may, I would marry Audrey.

The next day, in a pure Bollywood style, my dad said, 'Leave the house right now. You can't stay here any more. I don't want to keep any relationship with you.'

I left home, went to my brother's house, and then returned to Singapore.

Over the next few months, my mother kept asking me not to see Audrey any more because this would cause many problems within the family. I was in a difficult situation. I couldn't tell my parents that they could go to hell. I also couldn't tell Audrey that we shouldn't be together any more. I wanted to marry Audrey, but I also felt guilty about letting my parents down. I desperately hoped for a solution that could make both parties happy. It was no longer about my happiness.

Eventually, I tried to convince Audrey that we should stop our relationship. But Audrey insisted that I was the guy she wanted to marry.

Audrey: I became very upset with what Amit said. Then, we broke up briefly. But I didn't want to break up. I began praying a lot.

Amit: Because she was upset, I became even more unhappy. So after around six months, I realized I must be firm. And

I decided to go ahead. I told my parents that this was what would be and that I was fine if it took them time to accept us. A senior family member, whom my dad respected a lot, told him it was okay. This person said that he knew of an Indian guy who was married to an Indian girl, and when they went overseas, the wife couldn't adjust and eventually, they divorced. That despite the couple being both Indian, they had problems. My father was more accepting after that. My mother eventually came to Singapore to meet Audrey.

Looking back, I can perfectly understand my parent's strong reaction. It was such a strange concept. They felt they would be judged by society, that they would lose face, and that this would make them look bad. They didn't even get the idea of what a Chinese was. My mother asked me, 'Is she a Hindu or not?'

Audrey: My mother also said, 'You are the only grandchild of your grandfather. If you marry this boy, your kids will not be Chinese.' I said it is not like I am a king who owes the kingdom an heir.

Amit: It is some attachment deep inside that you feel strongly about. I, too, felt bad while giving up my Indian citizenship.

My parents had multiple layers of hopes, first, can you marry an Indian, if not, can she at least come to India and settle down here, if not, can your children be raised as Indians? Even now, my mother asks, 'Your son will eventually marry an Indian girl. Right?' And till now, my mother works hard to impress Audrey to move to India. She keeps telling Audrey how incredible India is—so many languages and all that.

So eventually, we got married, and it was just a regular affair. Some of my relatives attended our wedding in India, but some didn't—on purpose. But still, there were enough guests. Our marriage was the talk of the town, in my hometown of Hazaribagh.

Audrey: It even got into the newspaper. The first time I made it into the news, and it was in this Indian newspaper.

One thing my mother found very strange about Indian marriages was the practice of dowry. In China, it is the guy who pays the girl's family. For Indians, it is the other way. But in our case, we just didn't discuss the topic. The contrasting practices would have offset each other anyway.

Amit: If your mom expected any payment from me for this, then no way [laughs].

Audrey: We have been married for seven years now. We have a daughter and a son. We live like any other couple. But our different cultures affect our lives in certain ways. For example, when there are Diwali parties in the condo, we are not invited. If I try to connect to other Indian wives, some do not want to include me in their social circle. If I am talking to them, they may suddenly turn around when they see someone they know more. Amit gets upset because of this. He thinks that because he has a Chinese wife, he can't stay as connected to his culture as he should be. But I face the same issue. Some Chinese families just don't want to be close to us. So what can we do?

Amit: We do get left out of many social occasions. The atmosphere inside our home is also not very Indian any more. Now, we celebrate Diwali in a very small way, while back home in India, it is such a big deal. I miss this, just because I was born in that culture.

I do have a strong wish that our kids stay connected to Indian culture. I hope they will be able to find some sense of belonging. That is not easy; interracial kids may struggle to find their identity. Am I an Indian, a Chinese, or a Singaporean? If I were married to an Indian, there would be mostly Indian friends and families we would mingle with. We could then get more opportunities to immerse in that specific culture. It is not Audrey's fault, but just something that I wish for that is not easy to fulfil.

I try to take my kids to the temple on important occasions, even though I was never a religious person. For now, I put their identity as Hindu. All I want is for them to understand a concept like Hindu religion. I want them to know at least what a Hindu god looks like.

Audrey: I just tell my kids that you are Singaporeans because you were born here. As of now, our six-year-old daughter has no problem finding friends. And the other kids are okay with her as well. I just hope it stays that way. If one day the world is more connected, it will be much better for children of mixed lineages like ours.

Amit: In Singapore, it is okay because there are people from so many races. Our daughter has not yet asked how you two got married when you are Indian and mother is Chinese? She might ask when she is older, but that will be a part of growing up.

But there are other practical challenges of marriages like ours. When we go back to India, Audrey is often not comfortable.

Audrey: When I went to India for the first time, it was a big shock. I was still happy once we landed at the Delhi airport. We took the subway, and it was nice as well, there was even a separate compartment for the ladies. But when we got out on the streets of Old Delhi, it was so dirty. Cows were walking down the middle of the road—that was the biggest shock. And then we went to Agra by train and on the platform there, some guy had pooped, and I just stepped on it.

Amit: This was back in 2013, before we got married. She was quite traumatized.

Audrey: If I had visited in 2011 or 2012, I might have walked away. But by then, we were too close. But even now I have challenges. It is hard to be positive out there. If we go in summer, it is so hot. I can't wear skirts. There are all these protocols. I like to have a nice shower. But there, we only have buckets. In his hometown, the food, like the chicken, is sometimes not fresh. The milk there has so many lumps inside. In India, I cannot find toilet paper anywhere. Once we went to his brother's house, and when I flushed the toilet there, the bidet jumped off and the water—meant to clean people's bum—fell all over my face. I was crying so hard that day.

Overall, I am bothered by the personal hygiene practices of some Indians. Like when we had a birthday party for our daughter—during Covid days—some Indian parents fed her the cake with their hands covered with henna; they didn't even sanitize their hands. Also, when his mom is here, we sometimes have to discuss about cleanliness. On the other hand, my mom is very finicky about cleanliness.

Amit: Where I grew up—and I am not proud of this—a cockroach in the house was not a big deal [laughs]. But Audrey's reaction to a cockroach is very dramatic. She will clean the whole kitchen if she sees one.

Audrey: Just one cockroach means there could be a nest. Amit calls me the Cleaning Nazi [laughs]. But he doesn't even know where the mop is.

Another difference between Indian and Chinese is this 'do nothing' attitude that some Indians have. We Chinese are always 'action-oriented'. Like Amit has this habit of just lying down, idling, and checking the phone. But I just can't be like that. I think it comes from the culture, from the way Chinese mothers raise their kids—you must never waste time, and if you do, you are heavily criticized by your mother.

I also find that Indian men are not always treating women as equal partners. Like when Amit has a say, he wants me to follow. That is different from what I saw in China. My mom could have an equal conversation with my father; my grandparents, too, could have equal conversations with each other.

But Indians, in general, are more devoted to the family and more loyal to their partner than the Chinese. This is a big thing to me. My father always had a second life, separate from the family. He would keep many things hidden from my mother and me.

I also find Indian parents more accepting of their children's mistakes. Amit's parents are so kind and nice to me. Once, I took a long time to fill up a form at the airport, and they were so patient. This is the polar opposite of my mother. I was always so scared of her. My every mistake was heavily criticized. This is a common style of parenting in China.

Amit: The values in both countries are slightly different. My exposure to Chinese culture is only through Audrey. But in China, the values seem driven more towards achievement, like you must go to a more developed country. Perhaps Indians are less so in general; we are more family oriented.

Also, take the gifting culture in China. Gifts have a material value. If someone gives Audrey or us a gift, she thinks a lot about giving back something of bigger value. And if someone doesn't follow the protocol when it's our turn to receive gifts, she gets annoyed. But if I go to my friend's or their kid's birthday, I will not care much about the cost of the gift—just give them a $10 gift or just buy some toys as a goodwill gesture and write a nice message. Once during Audrey's birthday party, I gave her mom a smaller slice of the cake than the slice I gave my mom. That was the first time Audrey's mother complained.

But there are many good things about this marriage— Audrey's maturity, her logical thinking, the way she talks to me, the way she supports me. I wouldn't have all this if I married an Indian, or so I think. Also, because of our relationship, I have got exposed to many new things. This opens up new perspectives. I can make new types of friends.

Most importantly, I don't regret anything. It has been a very fulfilling marriage.

Audrey: All families have their problems. It depends on personalities and not where they come from. Even if it's an all-Indian or all-Chinese couple, they can all have problems.

Amit: Yes, if I look around, I see problems in every family. It is impractical to expect that marriage to be without any trouble. As for us, we live like any other married couple.

I don't interact with her relatives much, but all of them are nice to me. As for China as a whole, I only have good things to say. Of course, it is much more developed than India. I like Chinese food as well.

In the last few years, especially during Covid, there was much anti-Chinese talk in India. There are calls for a boycott of Chinese goods in India—a mass mentality created by politics. All these don't matter to me—maybe because I am not a nationalistic person. All that matters is that Audrey and I are okay with each other, that we take care of our family, and follow certain traditions from our respective cultures, that's all. I was indeed concerned if all this anti-Chinese talk would change my parent's perception of Audrey. But when we went back to India, no one mentioned anything. I think my parents don't look at Audrey as Chinese any more.

Our children look more Chinese than Indian. But I am not worried about their safety if they visit India. I just don't think they'll survive in India (if they were to move there). They can't. They'll always be treated as foreigners. That door is closed.

Audrey: During the border conflict, there was much anti-India stuff on Chinese media and social media too. People are easily manipulated—you are shown a thirty-second video, and instantly you make a conclusion about someone you have never met and start cursing them just because they live in another part of the world. This idea is ridiculous, and it's upsetting that people are so easily influenced.

Amit: Singapore generally has been accepting of our relationship. Sometimes older folks give us a look, but that's once in a blue moon.

Audrey: In Singapore, such racism is not in your face. Once in Paya Lebar, an old Indian man kept pointing his finger at us. Amit just asked him to go away. But once, when we were on a flight, a Singaporean lady who sat next to us asked, 'Do your parents even know?'

We Live in the China–India
New Village

Story of Connie Wang, thirties, Chinese–American born in China, and Vipin Jain, thirties, Indian from India. They are married and live in the United States of America

Connie: I grew up in Shanghai. Both my parents are college-educated and employees of large enterprises, used to travelling overseas for business. We also took many family holidays overseas. In my memory, my parents were always 'ahead of their peers' because of this international exposure. They supported me in studying in the UK and then in the US.

So I was surprised by their response when I announced that I was dating an Indian. My mother said, 'You are the sole purpose of my life. Now that your life is ruined, I might as well die or become a nun.'

She said I must have been abducted by an Indian and would be taken to India, where I would be raped. For two days, she refused to eat anything. She told me that I had hurt her very deeply. Concerned for her health, I lied to her. I told her that I had left Vipin.

Yet, we kept quarrelling for two years. We quarrelled every time we got on the phone. My parents were the same people who used to console their friends whose kids wanted to marry foreigners. They would tell them that it was okay. But then, these foreigners were mostly white or Japanese. When it was my turn, my mother even said it was better to find a lesbian partner than an Indian man. Despite knowing that Vipin and I were dating, my parents kept pretending I was single and still accepted people's referrals for dates for me. That is how I realized my parents were not really 'ahead of their peers' after all.

Vipin: I was born to a Jain family near Delhi. Jainism is a religion with many restrictions: we do not eat meat and many other foods. Since a young age, I was warned not to marry outside my caste. This restriction did not make any logical sense. But the more I was warned, the more I wanted to rebel against it. So once outside India, I dated people from different races, Spanish, Chinese, and others.

When I introduced 'the' Chinese girl, my family reacted strongly. They compromised from their earlier rigidity and said, 'At least marry an Indian girl.' Perhaps this resistance came from their lack of exposure. In India, our interaction with China is limited to two aspects: one, whatever happens at the border; two, Chinese goods.

Over time, my family stopped resisting, perhaps because I was getting older and they were worried that I would end up a bachelor. And now, my parents like Connie so much, especially for how she dedicates herself to what she wants to do.

Connie: I met Vipin on OkCupid. He was the first Indian I dated. I didn't like his photo, so I swiped it away. Despite my rejection, he sent me a message, 'If you like Xi'an Famous Foods restaurant (a Chinese restaurant in the US) or dumplings, we can still talk.' I liked his sense of humour. We met and became very attracted to each other. We shared a lot of common interests, such as a passion for food. Vipin eats meat though it's not officially known to his parents. He just doesn't cook meat. He said he was spiritual but not religious. I was the same. So I resonated with that.

Both of us are very rational people. So I told him frankly about my parents' bias, that it was unfair, and that I would understand if he chose to leave the relationship. But Vipin was calm and supportive. He was never aggressive or pushy. He told me we must slowly work through this and convince our parents.

I had studied intercultural conflict in a summer programme (my major was psychology though I am now an acupuncturist). So I applied my learnings to my own family. According to the theory, my family was at level one, the 'denial stage,' which is defined by 'perceiving people from different cultures in simplistic, undifferentiated, often self-serving ways.' I also got inspiration from doctors who treat allergies with exposure therapy: progressively increasing exposure to allergens. I decided to increase my parents' exposure to Indians and their culture. I knew my parents loved me. I knew they wanted me to be happy. I just needed to let them see the real person.

My mum refused to meet Vipin when she came to visit me in the US. So I got Vipin to come and help with her luggage when she was about to leave. I said there was no one else available to help. So they met for only five minutes. Years later, mum told me she 'liked him already' from those brief five minutes. His humble manners, courage to show up despite knowing he was not welcome, and determination to support me, completely changed my mum's prejudice.

My parents had been worried that I might 'become an Indian person.' So, they felt assured when they saw that I wasn't changing much. They also felt comforted seeing me happier than when I was single. They always said I had dated too few people before deciding on an Indian. After all, I studied in an all-girls high school followed by a women's college. But I had dated enough to know what I didn't want.

We held a simple wedding. Our parents attended via Zoom. We decided to invest money into a house instead of wedding rings. Both of us are practical people. Vipin had once taken me to an Indian wedding. While I felt excited about this new experience, we both agreed that we didn't want such extravagance for ourselves.

When I posted our couple photos on Xiaohongshu[9], some random people left nasty comments: 'Couldn't you find any better man?', 'Why must you marry an Indian?' Some commented that he was very dark. Some asked about his caste. Maybe this comes from how India is represented in Chinese media—it is always bad, rape cases and violence. Some media even make fun of India's National Day Parade—the Indians don't even have proper weapons.

Some of my relatives also asked my parents why I married an Indian. But my parents defended us. It was a complete turnaround. Of course, my parents still can't imagine us settling in India—they think our quality of life will worsen. But now they explain to all that our life is the same as same-race couples and that Indians are not what they are known to be.

Well, the reality is that there are unique challenges in our kind of marriage. Take food for example, Vipin loves Chinese food, and I love Indian food and even promote it among my friends. But his parents are very strict with their diet, so it is challenging when they come to live with us. There were times Vipin and I sneaked out of the house to get our meat fixes. I don't want our kids to be vegetarians without choosing for themselves, either.

---

[9] A social media platform in China, its name means 'little red book'.

But the fact is that there are many similarities between Indian and Chinese cultures. That's why Indian and Chinese migrants follow such similar paths in the US. Both work in high-skilled industries. Both believe in education. Often, both end up selecting the same neighbourhoods to live in. Where we live in the US is a classic example. It is in Jersey City, facing Manhattan across a river. Our place is nicknamed China–India New Village because both Indians and Chinese live here in abundance. There are even Chinese and Indian supermarkets.

Makes me wonder if it truly is that strange for these two races to congregate once they are outside.

Our Worlds Collided Effortlessly

Story of Mei Wan, thirties, Chinese–Australian, and Jay, thirties, Indian–Australian born in Malaysia. They live in Australia and are about to get married.

Mei Wan: I was born in Perth, Australia. My family came over in the eighties from Malaysia to Australia. They are all in the food business. We are one big crazy Asian family—three families and three generations in one household. At one point, we were seventeen people in the same house.

At home, we had a very traditional Chinese setting. My parents were quite strict. When all our friends were going for sleepovers, we weren't allowed to. But outside—our suburbs, my school—it was all very Australian. I was among the only two or three Asian kids in school. That was a challenge. We looked different, and we did different things. We were sometimes bullied in primary school because kids didn't know any better. I just wanted to fit in. So I assimilated to the norm—Western culture—and in my younger years, I pushed away Asian or Chinese traditions. We got our parents to pack us Western-style lunch—sandwiches—to not get picked on at school.

My parents are Hare Krishna devotees. We went to the Hindu temple, ate and cooked Indian food, and immersed ourselves in that culture. That made things even more complicated as I felt I was a mix of Chinese, Australian and Indian. And it was so hard to find vegetarian food in Australia in the early nineties.

Jay: I grew up in a small town called Segamat in Johore, Malaysia. We are Punjabi Sikhs. My father worked in a bank. My mother was the head of the English department at a Chinese high school. Because of her, all of us ended up in Chinese schools. In school, everyone could speak English, but they didn't want to. Kids can be mean, you know. So I had to learn Mandarin very quickly. The other kids wouldn't talk to me otherwise. People are shocked when they hear me speaking fluent Chinese. Back then, it was my fight for survival.

After I finished high school, my family moved to Australia. We assimilated well in Australia. This was because of the English language. On our very second day in Australia, I got a part-time job at KFC[10]. Many of their staff were from China. So I could still go on speaking Mandarin. And in Australia, I met more Punjabis than in Segamat. So my Punjabi, which was average in Malaysia, became very good.

Now, I work in the area of land development. I met Mei Wan because of our work. A friend of hers got us together to discuss a land development project. I actually talked Mei Wan out of it. Then we realized that most of our conversation was not about the development but about us.

Mei Wan: From my mid-twenties, I stopped running away from my Asian culture. By then, Australia had also become more multicultural. There was a lot more migration. I started having more friends from Asian backgrounds. So when I met Jay, we had such common ground. Both of us have Malaysian roots. So it was a beautiful point where I felt connected back to Asia, and I immersed myself back in it. I appreciated the East meets West synergy that pulled the best from both cultures.

---

[10] Kentucky Fried Chicken, a restaurant chain.

Jay: My family didn't object to our relationship. I was over thirty. So, my mom was very happy that I had someone. Indian parents are quite interesting, aren't they? When you are younger, they will be like no, no, no, no, no, no, no, you can't have a relationship. And then once you reach a certain age, suddenly they will be like, why do you not have anyone? What is going on? What's wrong with you? Moreover, my uncle is married to a Chinese. So my family is used to intercultural relationships.

Mei Wan: I didn't really face any resistance from my family either. My mum did question Jay being Indian at first. I always thought my mom—being very traditional—had probably wanted me to marry a Chinese person. But they are also Hare Krishna devotees and hang out with Indians. Also, Jay speaking in Mandarin with my family definitely earned extra brownie points for him.

My sister also married a Malaysian–Indian, and they have a beautiful Chindian son. So my sister was the guinea pig—the test case. They paved the way for us.

Anyway, it was important for me that my family accepted Jay for who he is. I always remembered my grandma saying, 'Make sure you find a good family because you are not just marrying that man, you're marrying his family.' And when I met Jay's family, it just felt so right.

Jay: She saw the chaos. I have three younger sisters, all in their twenties. They talk a lot.

Mei Wan: And the care they showed. Everyone was chill. No one took me for an outsider. It's just the Asian family way.

Jay: We introduced each other to our parents within three months. By month four, we had moved in together.

Mei Wan: Moving in before marriage was our biggest hurdle. It was like breaking a taboo. My mom, being very old school, wasn't very happy about it. She wanted us to get married first. I told her we would not get married until at least a year of living together.

Jay: I told my dad we were no longer in our twenties. We are not silly. I also told her mom that this is 2020. People need to know whether they can live with each other, that this is actually a good thing. But she still kept talking about it. Anyway, she has accepted it now. Other than that, we didn't face any challenges. But I was also shocked when Mei Wan asked if I wanted to move in. So I asked her twice to confirm if that's what she had said.

Between the two of us, it has been easy to adjust. There is a common Asian way of doing many things—like walking into a house, we will always take off our shoes before we go inside. Of course, there are personal quirks, but they are not cultural. My last relationship was with a Punjabi. Everything was the same for us—our culture, our religion. But it just didn't work out. So you need to be looking at what makes you happy.

Mei Wan: So, Jay loves Chinese food, and I love Indian food. So that works out. But I like Western food, and Jay is not that big of a fan. So we have to adjust that way.

So when we eat out, it is always Asian food. But I love cooking, so I often cook Indian food at home, like biryani and curries. Jay doesn't like chapatis, so it is easy for me that way. Some Indian women we meet at the temples complain that they must make chapatis for their husbands daily. I'm like, 'Oh, great, mine loves rice.'

It would, of course, have been great if we were from the same religion and went to the same temple. It would make

things easier. But we've adjusted to our differences. We go to
both temples.

Jay: We have many congregations—family events, weddings—
where cousins, parents, siblings, all come to the gurdwara at the
same time.

Mei Wan: Honestly, it is more convenient that way. They all
live far from each other and otherwise would be hard to meet.

Jay: She's been so many times to the gurdwara that everyone
knows who she is. The Hare Krishna part of Mei Wan's family
is new to me. So I'm learning. Every time I speak to her dad,
I learn something about it.

Mei Wan: We did a fire sacrifice ceremony when we first
got our house. We have planned for both our cultures to be
reflected in our wedding. Of course, the Punjabi side will show
more just because they have many more ceremonies related to a
wedding—*Sangeet, Maiyaan, Mehndi, Anand Karaj*, and all that
spread over four days. There will be a lot of dancing. It will be
wintertime, so it'll be less difficult.

So, we follow both Sikh traditions and Chinese traditions,
including a tea ceremony, and the Hindu Hare Krishna tradition.
So, we just double up on those things. This just means we need
more time. But it's beautiful.

Jay and I are open about how we will raise our kids when
they come. It's important to us that even though we live in
Australia, our kids understand that we also have a very rich
Asian culture and heritage that we shouldn't forget. It's quite
easy to forget one's culture and tradition when the majority are
Westerners who don't have strong traditions, family connections,
or religion as we do. So I've come full circle. I want to teach my

children about the Chinese culture my grandparents grew up with. Otherwise, it will get lost, and that thought makes me feel so sad.

Jay: When we have kids, they will surely speak multiple languages, and Mandarin and Punjabi will be among the languages that will be spoken.

Mei Wan: That's one reason I have been learning Mandarin. Because at home, we speak Cantonese. I can't even understand some things when Jay and my mother speak in Mandarin.

Jay: The kids will also have a Malaysian connection. There's still family there for both of us. We'll always go back once a year. We will always talk about our food which is the best in the world, and fight with Singapore over who has better food.

Politics aside, people in Malaysia are very nice. So Malaysia will always have a special place in our hearts. Even though the country didn't do anything for me when I needed it most, when people ask me, where are you from, I'll say Malaysia.

Mei Wan: I will say the same.

It was tough in my younger days. If I wanted to do something, my parents would say, 'No, you're not doing that.' I pushed the boundaries and rebelled, and they softened up as they became more comfortable with the Western way.

All along, I had thought I would end up with a Westerner. But in my later twenties, I accepted my Asian roots. So now I am content with this combination of East meets West. I see the value of Asian culture—the hard work ethic, the discipline, the devotion, the love for family and food. And then I love the Western side—the communication, the freedom, progressiveness, and the work hard, play hard attitude.

Hopefully, this fusion will transcend into us bringing up our kids in that way as well.

Jay: I am a 100 per cent Asian. I flaunt this fact.

In general, people in Australia have gotten used to intercultural couples and kids. Australia is so diverse, so multicultural, and it has been so for a long time.

Mei Wan: There are times when we have faced racism. During the early days of Covid, I could feel people sometimes walking away or steering clear of us and Chinese people or anyone looking Asian. You know when you feel someone's energy that way.

All this doesn't get us worried about our children. My cousins have mixed kids, and we see how well they fit in. But, again, this is because of how multicultural Australia has become. So we've got to equip them with the tools and resources to understand that they might be a little different, but they're perfect just as they are.

Jay: I've never considered it a huge issue because Australia is such a big melting pot. I never got bullied in Australia because I came when I was a bit older. My sisters were all fine because they were assimilated pretty well. I did get bullied in Malaysia, though—for the brief period I was in a Malay school—for being a Sikh because there were so few of us in Segamat. In Malaysia, they didn't have a box for Sikhs. So I always grew up in that box of 'Others'. But when you walk into a primary school here in Australia, you may have a kid who is Russian, Ukrainian, Afghani, Iranian, or Turkish, all in the same class, many mixed. That has become the norm. Of course, some kids will get bullied, for various reasons. That has to be handled in its own way.

Mei Wan: I am grateful that we have come together at a time we have, when our worlds could collide without much problem, and we can create our own type of culture and way of living. Just thirty or forty years ago, it might have been much harder for interracial couples like us. I feel very fortunate that we get to share amazing rich cultures, and strong traditions, and don't forget the delicious food and special moments with family and friends. When you get to the stage of appreciating and respecting your own culture and your partner's culture, a beautiful harmony is created. It feels effortless and is really priceless. Enjoy the journey and all the ebbs and flows!

IV

'Tradition is comprised of habits,' as astutely pointed out by Jayanta Meetei. Once the objections of the families have been overcome and the individuals from Chinese and Indian backgrounds have settled into their new life as a couple, they have to still make significant adjustments to navigate their divergent sets of habits.

From intangible aspects such as values, beliefs, communication styles, problem-solving approaches, and decision-making processes to more tangible elements like language, food habits, everyday intricacies, love, patience, and endurance are consistently put to the test.

As couples make substantial compromises and adapt to new circumstances, fairness can sometimes be threatened, compelling them to find a new sense of balance. Even simple tasks like operating a washing machine or going grocery shopping can suddenly become perplexing, leading us to ponder—like Lim Pei Ann in moments of despair—'Why did I make it so complicated?'

Inevitably, life becomes more complex for these couples. However, they often choose to stay united in fighting their differences. A 'bigger picture' dominates over 'small matters'. But do all small matters remain small?

VI

Our Biggest Challenge Is Day-to-Day Communication

Story of Demi Zhou Hua, thirties, Chinese, and Kumar Gupta, forties, Indian. They are married and live in Guangzhou, China.

Demi: I grew up in a small village in Hunan. As a child, I enjoyed singing, dancing, and reading. I also loved studying. But at sixteen, I dropped out of school and came to Guangzhou as a factory worker.

In the factory, I learned the basics of shoe-making: ladies' shoes, sports shoes, slippers, sandals, and boots. . .While working, I studied part-time, where I learnt English. Thanks to my English, I got an office job within two and a half years.

Kumar: I admire Demi. She has always been very independent and progressive. At such a young age, she made this big decision to drop out of school to support her family. And while she started as a factory worker, she first became a white-collar worker, then a merchandiser, senior merchandiser, manager, and then moved into operations and marketing.

I grew up in New Delhi. My mother comes from the Marwari community, and my father is from the Bania community, both communities well-known in India for their business acumen. Both communities are also very god-fearing, and therefore they condemn non-vegetarians.

After graduation, I worked in a garment business in India. A recruiter then contacted me for a managerial role in an Indian company's Guangzhou office. I had never heard of Guangzhou before. When I googled it, I realized it was a modern city with many buildings and factories. I also didn't know much about China except being a big fan of kung fu movies. I have watched every movie by Jackie Chan, from *Drunken Master* to *Shaolin Temple*.

People used to ask me, 'Why China? Why not America?' Most Indians knew little about China. They just see it as a restrictive communist country. Because of the China–India war and our irresponsible local media, many Indians have negative sentiments against China. But I decided to go to China. I was curious to learn about the country. I wanted to know how their businesses beat us so easily on price. I am an adventurer, I always jump into new things. Even today, I play various sports and read widely. I saw China as an adventure.

At first, I just wanted to spend a year or two in China. That was my plan. But look at me today. I have been in China for fifteen years. And I am now married to a Chinese girl.

I have always been very independent. Any decision about my life has to be mine. I was the first person in my clan to have a love marriage. All my siblings and cousins had arranged marriages. My first wife came from a different community, she was Punjabi. It should have been a big deal, but I didn't encounter much resistance. My family knows I am stubborn.

Soon after our wedding, my first wife joined me in Guangzhou. But we spent little time together. I was crazy busy at work. The business portfolio I took over was in a big mess. If you are devoted to work, the pace of China consumes you completely. We were also socially isolated. Eventually, our relationship fell apart.

I liked Guangzhou. It was safe and a lot more organized than New Delhi. I made friends with many expatriates. We hung out together. I had a good time there. It was a place where you could live longer. In China, I haven't experienced any racism. I have travelled to more than thirty cities, from Heilongjiang to Hunan, Hangzhou, Dalian, and Sichuan. Everywhere I found the people very polite and welcoming. Sometimes, they even attempted to speak a little English with me, 'How are you?

Things changed a bit during COVID-19. The media said that while Covid had vanished from China, foreigners were bringing it back. I noticed people avoiding me in the streets and restaurants. When I entered a lift, people would get out of it or turn their backs on me. It was as if I would eat them up. Very strange.

Demi: The media was also very irresponsible during the recent war between India and China. I was worried that people might hurt him. I asked him to keep his mask on in public. That way, he could be mistaken for a Pakistani or Arab.

My acquaintances also think Kumar is an Arab or Pakistani, never have they guessed him to be Indian. When I tell them the truth, they look disappointed. There is more comfort with Pakistanis because China greatly supports Pakistan. And Arabs sound richer than Indians. In general, the Chinese have negative impressions of Indians. However, most of them haven't met any Indians in life. As a mixed couple, we attract stares from people, especially when I was pregnant. I wasn't too bothered about it.

Kumar: If it is a female, they'll stare at me first and then at her. It's the other way for men. My theory is: the women are jealous of her. And the men are jealous of me.

Demi: I, too, had a terrible impression of Indians. Once, an Indian man contacted me on the internet. He was studying at a university in China. I agreed to meet him to learn more about his university—I had never been to any. He was late, stingy, and touchy-feely.

My first meeting with Kumar was also not great. He had interviewed me at my previous company. He made me wait for three and a half hours! I concluded that Indians were always late.

Kumar left three months after I joined the company. Rumour had it that he had returned to India to save his marriage. He came back three years later. I was still there, even though I hated my boss, Kumar's successor.

Kumar: The business had performed terribly under my successor. Clients weren't happy with his working style and execution. So the company courted me with a bigger role and pay package. Since I had already closed the chapter with my ex- wife and had no other life plans, I took the offer and returned to Guangzhou.

Demi: By then, I had been promoted to senior merchandiser. I was also pregnant with my first kid with my ex-husband. Kumar made me work hard. But he always asked about my and my baby's health. He has a good heart. If he wanted me to attend a meeting, he would say, 'If it's inconvenient for you to take public transportation, you can take a taxi. The company will pay for it, or I will pay for it.' I was touched.

Kumar: We worked closely together for five years. She was one of my key people. She was intelligent and had opinions, unlike ninety per cent of Chinese who don't have any and are just waiting for your opinion. She opened my eyes to new possibilities. This was refreshing. I started involving her outside her functional area. She could simplify complex problems, cut away the fat, and understand the issue's essence for me to solve. I also learned many things about China through her. We had a mutual admiration and liking for each other.

Demi: Both of us love work. We worked together and travelled together extensively. We also fought a lot, because of our different opinions and work styles.

Indians work very differently from the Chinese. The managers in that Indian company were all Indians. I could never count on their verbal commitments. To deal with this Indian style, I had a few tactics. As much as possible, I pursued them to sign documents. I insisted on clear 'yes or no'. After every meeting, I emailed them to recap every detail and hold them accountable. I worked with Kumar in the same way: always asking for written confirmation when I needed his approval. In the eyes of my colleagues, I was this strict and headstrong Chinese lady.

Indians are also very inefficient. They are never on time. A half-an-hour meeting with them lasts two hours—they never focus on the real agenda. All this led to many arguments.

Kumar: The Chinese and Indians work very differently indeed. I had communication issues with them. If a Chinese says yes, take it as a no. Even if they have not understood me, they say yes just to end the discussion. Initially, I was very frustrated. But I had no way out but to learn to cope. I discussed every matter three times. Then I would check their understanding. After that, I would explain further and check their understanding again. With this, I formed a habit of repeatedly explaining and checking everything, even in a family context. So Demi sometimes gets angry with me. This inefficient over-communication has become a part of me.

Chinese people follow processes diligently and meticulously. If you give them a process chart, they will complete every step flawlessly. They need little supervision. But we Indians don't care about processes and systems. We improvise at every step, bending and moulding rules, to do things our way. Each approach has its benefits.

In our own lives, Demi is very process-oriented, and I am more strategic. I always seek to understand a problem deeply, get to the root cause and take measures to prevent future incidents.

Demi: But every meeting has a different agenda, duration, and audience. Why do strategic stuff in routine meetings? Why go beyond the purpose of a meeting? The same medicine can't cure all problems.

I was drained working with so many Indians. So every year, I sent a resignation letter to Kumar, copying HR. But then he would hand me a promotion, a salary increment, and pitch great career prospects. And he delivered on all his promises. I carried on.

But once we began dating, I felt uncomfortable working in the same company and reporting to him. I asked him, 'Do you love my work or me as a person?' I was confused. So eventually, I made a brave decision to leave the company. Until today, he hasn't found a proper replacement.

Kumar: Demi will always be the best.

Demi: It was one such resignation letter that eventually got us together. I had just gotten divorced. The divorce hurt me so much that I decided not to marry again.

Kumar: This was three years before we got married. I knew she had gone through a breakup. So I invited her and another colleague to India. Although she didn't seem heartbroken, I thought a trip might benefit her.

Demi: I just didn't show my true feelings. I just wanted to work, make money, live, and enjoy the way life is. I suspected getting me to India was part of Kumar's strategy to retain me.

It was my first trip to India. A friend had advised me to cover myself fully while in India. Conscious of my fair skin, I packed clothes that showed as little skin as possible. But in Delhi, I saw the women dressed just like us, very modern, some even wearing very low cuts.

Kumar: I don't know who briefed her about India being difficult for females. Delhi was very hot at that time, around thirty-five degrees Celsius. She wore a velvet jacket and tracksuit! I said, 'You will get roasted!'

Demi: India was better than I had imagined. We always had a car and a driver with us; he made us feel very safe. Probably, I didn't experience the real India. But I saw the Taj Mahal, and I saw the poor and the rich. I also experienced Indian hospitality.

We stayed at Kumar's house. I really envied his family. They looked so happy, very different from mine. When I was young, my parents fought a lot and later divorced. They hardly spent any time with me. But Kumar spent time with his sister, niece, and parents. I saw how close he was to them. I married him because of this family. A man with such a nice mother and sister wouldn't be that bad.

I had a culture shock when I saw young people touching their elders' feet. I did this to his father a few times. Even though Kumar said I didn't have to be so formal, I didn't want to be seen as rude.

I didn't like the Indian habit of eating late. Dinner only starts at 9 p.m. and finishes at 11 p.m. Parties start at 11 p.m. and finish at 3 a.m.

Kumar: That's the culture. We believe in enjoyment and companionship. Food is not so important to us. In China, food gets too much emphasis. When you visit someone's house, some elder will call you, 'Where are you? The food is getting cold. Come quickly.' In India, we will just ask, 'Where are you? When will you arrive? We'll prepare food accordingly.'

Food habits are also very different in the two countries. In China, you always serve freshly cooked food. Then you use your chopstick to pick from all dishes. In India, cooked food is kept in big casseroles and different serving spoons are used for different dishes.

Demi: In India, the same cooked food is cooked many times. In China, the food is only cooked once. It tastes better when fresh. The taste changes if the food turns cold or gets reheated. My mother gets very angry when the food is on the table, and he shows up half an hour later.

Indian food doesn't look healthy. But they do eat many good things, like walnuts, chia seeds, flax seeds, and turmeric.

Kumar: Once, when Demi cooked in our house, she finished half a can of oil in one go. My mother was shocked. She could have cooked six meals with the same amount of oil. She wondered how Chinese people could stay thin when they eat so much oil. I never told Demi this, but my mother found the food flavourless. 'Where are spices?' she asked. Demi couldn't use garlic because we didn't eat much of it in our house. I enjoyed the food, I knew how to appreciate Chinese food. My family didn't.

Demi: We stay slim because we eat in small quantities. We cook with a lot of oil but eat only the food, not the oil. Indians eat a lot of curry with oil in it. In that sense, Indian food is more oily.

Kumar: Also, my family is strictly vegetarian. My mother has never even eaten an egg. I never ate meat at home, but I started eating it outside since very young. My mother was not happy. She used to blame this for my weight gain.

During that first trip, after two days of eating vegetarian fare at my house, Demi asked me, 'Do you only eat this?' Then I took them to a restaurant for chicken tikka. I don't see us becoming vegetarian ever, especially Demi. She won't consider it in her next five lives.

In China, I used to have an Indian cook. A month after Demi moved into my house, the cook was gone. Since then, I've been eating only Chinese food at home. Because of this, I used to crave Indian food. But that craving has gone away on its own.

Demi: Only because he realized that Chinese food is healthier [laughs].

Kumar: I'm not sure what the reason is. But, indeed, I have always liked Chinese food. Now we live like a proper Chinese household. There is no multi-nationality over here. My mother-in-law lives with us. So our way of living is more Chinese.

After a few months of living together, we decided to get married. We planned an engagement party and a wedding party in India. We even booked our tickets, including for Demi's little girl, who had already met my family. But then Covid happened, and we couldn't go anywhere. Since Demi was pregnant, I informed my parents we would just get married in China.

Demi: All his relatives and friends couldn't understand why he married me—a divorced Chinese woman with a child. One of his cousins lost his temper; he doesn't talk to Kumar any more.

On my side, marrying him was less of an issue than my divorce. A divorce is a big deal in the small village I grew up in. But those people's views were none of my concern. And if I could find a good partner after the divorce, why not? I knew marrying an Indian would be an adventure. My husband has a very kind heart. This gave me the courage to go on this adventure.

Kumar: We held a simple party in a park. We invited just a few friends. She wore a black dress and sports shoes. I wore a jacket, a shirt, and pants. We exchanged rings. Then we all went for dinner. That was at the peak of Covid. A maximum of ten people were allowed in restaurants.

We kept everything simple, thinking we could have a proper wedding soon after Covid was over. Three years have gone past. We don't know how things will be, but we will definitely hold a wedding party.

Kumar: Demi was in two minds about her five-year-old daughter living with us. The girl was then living with Demi's mother, about 100 kilometres from us. Demi was very attached to her daughter and found every chance to be with her. Could I truly accept the child? We can get an easy answer on humanitarian grounds. But it is not so easy when it is a life choice. After some deep thinking, I realized that unless the daughter lived with us, I would have a half-filled Demi and a half-filled home. So I pushed Demi and ensured we all lived together.

Demi: Both of us are new to parenting. Kumar has lived alone for many years. And I, too, didn't live with my elder daughter for all these years. Since my elder daughter was not born of him, I can be very sensitive to Kumar's attitude to her. He cannot speak Chinese, and my older daughter speaks limited English.

But Kumar loves kids and is trying hard to be a good father. He spends as much time with the kids as he can. He comes home early, especially after our child was born.

We always argue over kids' studies. As a full-time housewife, I have to manage their studies, the food, and also have to play with them. I have to do all the grocery shopping. Kumar can't help me even if he wants to. His life in China relies a lot on me because of the language issue. So I often feel overwhelmed and become emotional.

Kumar: Demi is a very nice person. She has a pure heart. But our biggest challenge is day-to-day communications. Chinese people tend to focus on tasks, not people. As such, they don't prioritize emotions or deep conversations, unlike Indians. We also have very different upbringings. I come from a family with close ties, while her family has more silos. My family is male-dominant, while hers female-dominant.

Demi: Our differences in habits and communication styles stem from our cultural differences. My limited English capability is also an issue. But indeed, it's also from different upbringings. He comes from an affluent family in India, while I am an ordinary village girl. I find him longwinded, while he finds me too direct.

Every morning, when he leaves home, he wants to hug and kiss me. But I get annoyed by this loving act because I want to get to the next thing on my to-do list. Domestic life can become so mundane and stressful that I can't see this romantic side. I know he is a good husband. I just need to prioritize him a little at such moments.

Our relationship is delicate. It needs extra care.

Why Did I Make Life
So Complicated?

Story of Lin Pei Ann, fifties, Taiwanese, and Chongtham Jayanta Meetei, fifties, Indian. They are married and live in Taiwan.

Jayanta: I was born in Imphal, in the north-eastern Indian state of Manipur. We were four siblings. My mother died when I was only thirteen. We siblings had to cook our own food thereafter. Being the eldest, I had to be the one managing the house. We were poor. I studied in a government school where there were no tables or chairs even. We had to bring along our own mats to sit on.

Manipur is a multicultural place. I am a Meitei. I am from the plains. But the tribal villages in the hills were just a thirty-minute walk away. We had many tribes, Muslims, and other different people. So when I came to Taiwan, I didn't find the cultural differences too shocking.

Yet, those were turbulent times in Manipur. The insurgency was going on. Back then, we all thought we were not part of India. We Manipuris have a strong identity. We feared that the government would give away our land to outsiders. Everybody wanted to join the rebels. When Bisheswar, an insurgency leader, was arrested, the Indian army used helicopters to drop pamphlets over our school to announce this. All of us students cried. Our family was Hindu, and we Meitei had Hindu names like Singh or Sharma. But all of us in our generation then changed our names to Meitei names. From Jayanta Singh, I became Jayanta Meetei.

While growing up, I watched many *jatras* (folk theatre). Watching them, I wanted to become an actor too. I dreamt of performing before a big crowd. When I was twenty-five, I dropped out of a master's programme in history to join the National School of Drama in Delhi.

In Delhi, I didn't face much racism like some north-easterners face within India. My classmates were all very good. But once I had a big fight. I was drinking tea in a small shop just outside the campus. A man called me 'Ei, Bahadur,' a slang used for Nepali security guards. I was not offended by what he said but by the tone with which he said it. I said, 'Hey, don't speak this way.' Four people surrounded me and started roughing me up. Someone alerted my classmates, and they rushed in to help me. They came with all the props. The police came soon and set us apart.

Other students from the north-east also faced problems. Once, a Manipuri student cooked dry fish inside the hostel. It has a strong smell. Other students scolded him badly. But we Manipuris can't do without dry fish. This is our food. Once, a student asked me how could we Manipuris eat bamboo. 'Don't your teeth break?' But we only eat the shoots. We are not pandas. Things in India have improved since then. Still, there are racist comments towards north-east people. So I feel safer in Taiwan than in Delhi.

Pei Ann: I was born in a small town called Miaoli in Taiwan. I am the middle child among three siblings. My parents were government officers. My father was always away from home because of work. So I didn't want to create any problems for my mother. I was very disciplined and responsible. I always handled things by myself. I didn't want my parents to ever worry about me.

In my whole life, I did only two things outside my parent's expectations—joining the theatre and marrying an Indian.

In Miaoli, we were all Hakka people. The only foreigners I saw were those few missionaries from the US. They used to greet us in their accented Chinese, '*Ni hao ma?*'(How are you?) or '*Ni xiang lai wo de jiaohui ma?*' (Do you want to come to our church?) I actually thought they were speaking English to me. So I thought English was a very easy language. You just need to change a bit the way you speak Chinese and then it becomes English. As a child, I never saw a real Indian. My parents sometimes referred to Indians as 'Indu Asan', a teasing way of talking about them.

I have been attracted to the theatre since my university days. I loved that on stage, I could become someone else. But I always only got the role of a mother, different types of mothers, but always mothers. My parents were not very pleased with my decision to join the theatre. I told them, 'If you don't support me, at least don't worry about me. I will survive by myself. But promise me that you will come to watch my performances.'

Then I got admitted to a theatre programme in Singapore. That was the first time I got heavily exposed to different cultures. All of us students from all parts of the world had to live together, study together, and practice together. That is where I met Jayanta.

Jayanta was different from the others. He was so charming on stage. He seemed so pure, so humble. I was attracted to that. We used to think Indian men were very dominating to women, but Jayanta listened to me. He would still argue, but together, we could find a reasonable solution.

Jayanta: I was struck by how independent Pei Ann was. I was attracted to it. But I also wondered if I should really pursue a relationship with such a strong character. I was not used to women being like her, even though Manipur is more liberal than the rest of India. In Manipur, over ninety per cent of marriages are love marriages, not arranged. We also practice eloping, where the girl runs away with the boy, and then his family visits the girl's family to ask for her hand. But even though Manipuri women have more rights, they are still dependent on men. It is always the men who make the decisions. So it was not easy for me to adjust to Pei Ann.

My thinking changed over time. What I had perceived as stubbornness was actually her individuality. The girl is also an individual. I am also an individual. That means we have to negotiate. We have to find common ground to agree on something. But sometimes I do feel greedy and think that if I had been married to someone from my society, I would have to compromise less, and I would be more in control. I am a human being after all.

Pei Ann: We are Hakka people. Our women are strong-minded.

Another obstacle to our relationship was his age. His passport says he is two years younger than me. I didn't want to be in a relationship with a *didi* (means younger brother but is also a term used to refer to a younger man). But one day— in the subway—he revealed that his actual age was different.

Jayanta: You know, in India, the real ages are all messed up. I am actually two years older than her.

Pei Ann: We got separated when Jayanta left Singapore two years into the course. I came back to Taiwan a year after. I thought that international relationships were transient like that. But then I visited him in India, and we travelled around. And we met again in Japan when we were both invited to a festival.

Jayanta: That coincidental meeting in Japan was a significant milestone for us. Before that, we saw little chance of us ending up as a married couple. In Japan, we got to be together for a long time—forty-five days. That's when we began thinking that this relationship had some potential.

Soon thereafter, I came to Taiwan for six months to prepare for another festival. Before that, I knew so little about Taiwan. I didn't understand the language. But when in Taiwan, I found that the people were welcoming. So I could then imagine the possibility of settling down here. In any case, Pei Ann and I were not getting any younger either. Then suddenly, she said, 'Let's get engaged in December.'

Pei Ann: Hello! Excuse me. Was it me who said that? Don't say that. You are not writing a script now.

Well, I did want to get the engagement done soon. My father was diagnosed with cancer. So I wanted to get this done. But this discussion happened after we had already agreed to get married. It remains a mystery who among us first proposed marriage.

Jayanta: Okay, since I am the man, let me say this time that it was I who proposed.

Pei Ann: My family was still in a state of shock when Jayanta and I invited them to a restaurant to announce our decision to get married. My parents had guessed I was going with him because of my trips to India. But they didn't know for sure. And they never expected me to marry a foreigner.

Jayanta: They said, 'Look, think again. Because love is different from marriage.'

Pei Ann: I was lucky that my parents left it to me to decide. One reason my family accepted Jayanta was that he sounded like a village boy. My parents grew up in the fifties and sixties when Taiwan was agricultural. Jayanta is familiar with that kind of society because Manipur is still like that. He and my parents could relate to each other. So, in essence, my parents wanted me to get married to a village boy.

Jayanta: The first time I met her mother, she said, 'He is okay. He is not so dark.'

Pei Ann: Earlier, my mother had said, 'Show me some photos of the guy before you make a decision. Our neighbour's daughter married an Indian. When they met their son-in-law at the airport, she fainted at the first look at him. The boy was so dark. I don't want to faint as well.'

Even when I was pregnant, my mother would joke, 'Will your baby look like a zebra? Black and white stripes?'

Jayanta: Initially, we lived with her parents. It was hard for all parties. They didn't say anything directly. But I could sense it. It is natural because they have not experienced any culture other than their own. So whenever they saw me doing things differently, they would wonder why. Like in Manipur, we never drink alcohol in front of our elders. Here, you drink together. Not just drink but say cheers loudly. I was very uncomfortable with that. So they would wonder, why didn't he say cheers? Then, it was natural for me to eat with my hands. The food was just not tasty if I ate with chopsticks. My daughter picked up this habit as well. The parents considered this very impolite. They would then say, 'See, the daughter has picked up Indian habits.' That hurt. Even if I knew they were speaking from the perspective of their culture.

For the first three years, I was really frustrated. I had no friends, no social circle. When I spoke English, others felt scared. Some didn't respond. I couldn't participate in anything about daily life. I was so dependent on Pei Ann for everything. I found it so hard to survive. I wanted to run away.

I survived because of theatre. It helped me pick up the language. When I wrote a script, it was translated into Chinese for the performance, and I had to follow each line as they were being spoken by the actors—during the multiple rehearsals and during the actual show. In three to four years, I spoke very much like a local.

Pei Ann: His Mandarin is quite good now. I have to switch to Hakka if I have to keep any secret from him.

Jayanta: Also, I had a very good realization that has helped me survive. This realization is that tradition is nothing but habits built over time. Therefore, no tradition is fixed. It is just a way of life you have got used to. I must respect that and not compare traditions all the time. I must also not get fixated on my own ways of doing things.

Say, in Manipur, girls having periods are not allowed to cook or touch other's utensils. The men cook during those times— that's why all Manipuri men are good cooks. This practice has some scientific reasons—hygiene or allowing the woman to rest. But people can get extremely fixated on it. My friends back in Manipur—all well-educated—won't even touch the food if their wives having periods have accidentally touched the utensil. They think the whole month will be unlucky for them. Such attitudes no longer have any scientific rationale. Instead, it becomes a radical perspective. This understanding helped me not to be fixated on my way of doing things. I was then willing to compromise and adapt to some of Pei Ann's family's habits. I will eat with my hands if I feel like it. If we are in a gathering where everyone is using chopsticks, I will also do the same. I will respect everyone, but I will also respect myself.

Or take my habit of drinking milk tea every morning. She doesn't like milk tea. She prefers Chinese tea. So I adjusted my habit; I don't have to drink milk tea daily. We can alternate between the two. We have to respect each other's choices and negotiate. Otherwise, such seemingly small things can cause big problems.

Let's take another case. I don't believe in god. I am an agnostic. So earlier, it was uncomfortable to go to the temple with Pei Ann's family. Sometimes their prayers and ceremonies can take really long. What do I do when they throw fortune sticks? What do I do when they pray? I can't simply follow them when I don't believe in them. We had arguments—why must I go to the temple?

Pei Ann: These occasions are very important to my family. Jayanta would be very moody before these. Initially, he would say he would come. My mother would cook special foods expecting him. Then the day before, he would change his mind. So we had arguments. I would say that I will skip all important days for you if we are in India. We also don't celebrate any special days—birthdays, wedding days, Valentine's day. Because he doesn't want to.

Jayanta: But after this realization about traditions came to me, I understood I could go to the temple just to give company to my wife and daughter, who believe in such practices. Going to the temple is a choice I can make to keep my family happy. When they pray, I now use the time there to meditate by being aware of my breathing. The temple then becomes the place to remind me that my life is my own doing.

Regarding rituals and days like birthdays, I have changed as well. I still don't like rituals. But now I understand that rituals have another purpose—to bring people together. So it is okay to celebrate some days in a minimalist way.

All these changes in my mindset happened because of theatre. Theatre forces you to be exposed to human nature. Both of us can't be involved in theatre without understanding human nature. Maybe that's why our marriage is a little different from other intercultural relationships.

Pei Ann: I understand that Jayanta has had to make many adjustments. It is not easy for him to live away from one's own culture in a completely different setting. Earlier, he used to be like the wild horse—who can't be controlled by anybody. Back in college, he never booked the rehearsal rooms, and others would get annoyed by it. But out here, he has to follow so many rules.

In comparison, I spent much less time in India. Even then, I had challenges adjusting. The first Manipuri phrase I learnt was 'What did you eat?' Everyone was asking that, almost as a greeting. 'How was the taste?', 'Was it good?' Why do they ask such things? They always complain that I eat too little rice. 'Why is the rice not occupying the whole plate like a mountain? This girl must then be very sick.' All this was new to me.

Then, there is the Manipuri custom of sharing—food, utensils, everything. Back in Taiwan, all of us in the family had our own cups. We even had our names written on them. But when we meet people in Manipur, all the cups are on the ground. Everyone is sharing. When we cook chicken there, one bowl has to go to this neighbour, another to another. In the end, there is little left for us. I was not used to such practices.

Now I understand that for any special dish, I just have to cook larger portions.

When I am in Manipur, I sense that people in his family get worried that I am angry.

I may indeed appear so. If I want to just go out to the nearby market, they will be like, 'Oh, you want to go out. Let's find that auto-rickshaw driver and see if he is available.' Someone they trust. I am frustrated by that. I am an independent person. Why can't I just take a scooter and go by myself? Why does such a simple thing need to be so complicated?

Jayanta: In Taiwan, everything is convenient. In Manipur, everything is inconvenient.

Pei Ann: Or say, if I can't finish my food, I would just ask Jayanta to finish it. In Manipur, that is a no–no. What is this? And why can't he pick up my clothes from the laundry since he is going there anyway? Why do they need to have separate utensils to cook chicken, and then those have to be kept outside the house?

Jayanta: We Manipuris are vegetarians on most occasions. So when we cook chicken, it has to be done outside. Also, in Manipur, the husband shouldn't eat his wife's leftovers. The husband cannot touch a wife's clothes. Or when men talk, women shouldn't talk. So when we are in Manipur, I am always conscious of such things. There, I am always worried that being a foreigner, she may do something different from local practices, and that would embarrass my family.

But people in Manipur always like it if we marry someone from Southeast Asia instead of India. Still, in their minds, they cannot accept that Manipur is part of India. Also, the culture from Southeast Asia appears similar. But initially, my family had no idea where Taiwan was. When I first told them about Pei Ann, they said, 'Oh, from Thailand!'

Pei Ann: But there are also similarities between Manipur and Taiwan. We have the issue with China; Manipur has the issue with India. For both of us, our sense of our unique identity is strong. But it is hard for me to explain to a Taiwanese person all these aspects of how diverse India is.

As for our daughter, since we live here, the Taiwanese influence is much stronger. But at some point, we want to send her for three or four years to India so she understands that part of her roots.

Jayanta: Here, when people ask about India, the questions come from an idea of India from the fifties and sixties. They ask about caste, poverty, and recently, rape cases. In the beginning, this was irritating. I had to explain every time, 'India is very big. This place is somewhat different, that place is somewhat different.' Or sometimes, they are just being curious. They ask, 'Oh, the Indians eat by hand. Don't your hands get burnt?'

But I didn't experience any real racism in Taiwan. Moreover, interracial marriages are on the rise in Taiwan.

Pei Ann: You can say that because you don't know the real story. Here, strangers often think Jayanta is a migrant labourer. Once, when we went to a shopping mall to buy him trousers, the staff said, 'Oh, you are so nice, you even buy clothes for your workers.' I said, 'Yes, he works very hard.' Some think he is an aborigine. If someone marries a foreigner who is not a white person, people here think that this is because she couldn't find anyone else. But with us, it is different, they assume we got married because of our common profession.

In Taiwan, when people hear my husband is a foreigner, they say, 'Oh, so cool!' It is not cool at all. When our friends see us, they see only harmony. But they don't see the tensions behind it all.

Sometimes I feel tired. I feel there is too much responsibility on me—because of my marrying a foreigner. Let's say a simple thing like driving. Jayanta can't read the signs in Chinese, so it is always me who is driving. During childbirth, my hospital room was so cold. But he couldn't operate the air-condition remote— all instructions were in Chinese. At that time, he couldn't even cook the rice at home—all cooker instructions were in Chinese. I had to draw a picture of the rice cooker for him. Earlier, he couldn't speak any Chinese either. The phone is ringing, why can't he pick it up? He was so scared because the person on the line only spoke Chinese.

For the same reason, I had to attend every social outing by myself. He wouldn't join. We cannot achieve such simple missions without issues. So sometimes I wonder, why? Why did I make my life so complicated?

Then, Jayanta's humbleness occasionally comes across as being meek. Like, setting up a theatre company in Miaoli is not easy. So, unless I stood determined to get things done, it wouldn't have happened. But also, sometimes, my ego becomes too strong and hinders good decision-making. That's when Jayanta comes across as a teacher and makes me see things differently. I am short-tempered. He is very calm and steady. So we are like yin and yang. He is the man, but he has the softness. I am the woman, but I have the hardness.

Slowly, I have learnt to handle such issues. It was my own decision, after all. I have accepted that some simple things will just take longer for us. I have become more patient. Yet, these are also practical challenges of marrying a foreigner.

Jayanta: So this is my message to all couples—not just interracial ones. Look at each other as individuals and understand that differences arise because of individual characteristics and habits—culture is just one such habit. We have to look beyond such habits. There is, of course, a social and cultural context behind everyone the way he or she is. For such contexts, we just have to learn to be careful and aware so we don't entertain racist feelings against one another.

Problems will never end. Even if I have a different partner, we will have problems. So we have to work through the problems. And I am very curious about how these problems arise from our cultural differences. Then, solving such problems become more interesting. Living in such an intercultural relationship enriches me more. I can understand myself better. I can discover myself in the process.

Pei Ann: Once we went back to Singapore. Our teacher asked, 'How can you stay together for twenty-four hours—at home, at the theatre?' It's a valid question. But until now, I don't feel bored with Jayanta. That has been the key to our relationship lasting for over eighteen years. As my teacher, he always has something new to give me. Even when we fight, I seldom think about breaking the relationship. I ask myself—if this person disappears, will it matter to you? My answer is yes.

When we got married, as per Indian custom, we tied the red strings in our hands and promised that we would stay together until we died. So until it becomes impossible to be together, we have to fight and find a way.

He's a Vegetarian. Are You Sure?

Story of Huiyi (name changed), thirties, Chinese, and Nemish (name changed), thirties, Indian. They are married and live in Canada.

Huiyi: My childhood friend gave a speech at our wedding. She said that when I was only twelve, I had already declared my wish to marry a foreigner. I had completely forgotten this. But it was true. I had a bad impression of Chinese men. Foreigners represented better qualities.

I come from a small city in Guangdong province, where ninety-five per cent of the people are Hakka. We are a conservative community. Many Hakka men did no housework and were not loyal to their partners. The women had to take care of everything, the house, the children, and the elderly, on top of a day job. Since young, I witnessed the struggles of the women in my family.

My fantasy about foreigners came from *Harry Potter* and *High School Musical.* The English language is so sexy.

My mother, too, loved English. But she wasn't given the opportunity to learn it when young. So she wanted to realize her dreams through me. My mother got me immersed in English books, movies, and songs. She even got me a private English teacher. He was an African–American, the first real foreigner I had met.

Nemish: I grew up in Chennai. It is more conservative than Mumbai or Delhi. People there are mostly vegetarians. There was no partying, and the few clubs there closed by 11 p.m.

My grandparents were uneducated village dwellers. My parents were the first to live in a city. My dad is a law professional, and my mom, a bank clerk. She could have been more successful but sacrificed her career for the sake of our education. I come from a lower-middle-class family. But my parents put our education above all. We didn't have a TV. My parents saved up to buy us a computer instead. It was a luxury back then.

My mother was progressive. Because of her, my brother and I are what we are today. Regarding my marriage, she said, 'You pick your own girl.' For Indians, marriage is between two families, not between two individuals. But my mom was clear that it would be my choice. And while my parents are Hindus and strict vegetarians, they didn't enforce religion or food restrictions on us. I studied in a Catholic school because it was considered better than others.

Growing up, we celebrated Deepavali and Ramadan equally. I had friends from all religions. Only now, I realize that it was a big deal.

I came to Singapore for a master's degree. At first, my friend circle was all Indian. But over time, I made friends with people from other races. Being an extrovert, I was often the first to reach out to others. This happened at my workplace too, where I was the only Indian in a very cosmopolitan team.

Then, Huiyi joined the same company, but in a different team. On her first day, we left work at the same time; we shared the same elevator down. We walked, we crossed the road, we went to the same station, and then we took the same train . . . all this without saying a single word to each other. This happened for a few days. I decided to end this awkwardness. I said 'Hi' in the elevator.

We became friends. This is how it all started.

Huiyi: I was a shy person. I hung around Chinese people because I thought my English was bad. Nemish was like the sun in my life. He warmed me up. He said, 'Your English is perfect, just speak up. You are doing great.' That gave me the courage. He brought me to meet new friends. Thanks to him, I became confident about meeting people from different cultures.

Nemish: My friends used to tease me that I prefer Chinese over Indian girls. I used to counter them. I believe the 'real' person mattered more than anything else, such as race. But I might actually have had a preference. I never dated any Indian girls, even though I had many friends among them. I found them cheerful but close-minded. Being open-minded is very important to me.

It's funny. I was looking for an open-minded person. But Huiyi wasn't one back then. But I liked how she was 150 per cent committed to whatever she decided to do. Also, her heart was so pure. It came through even in our brief interaction. This was, perhaps, most important for me then. Besides, there was a mutual physical attraction.

On our first date, I took her to try south Indian vegetarian food. Not having any meat in a meal was very new for her.

Huiyi: I was already nervous before going to the restaurant. And when I saw the food, I was shocked. I asked myself, 'What are those things?' Yet, I forced myself to swallow everything and said, 'This was pretty good.' I was only being polite. I had never eaten so many spices in my life! There was no meat!

Nemish: Then she said, 'Well, I really don't know where to treat you back. There's no Chinese place where you can eat.'

So she invited my roommate and me to her home and cooked Chinese vegetarian food for us.

Huiyi: I fried tomato with eggs, mushroom, cabbage and chillies. Nemish's roommate gave him a strange look as he swallowed the mushrooms. A few months later, this roommate told me that Nemish doesn't eat mushrooms.

Nemish: There was also this incident when we were all eating together in a food court. My roommate was shocked, 'Wait, her chopsticks dug into the meat dish and then into your vegetarian stuff. How are you fine with it?' I said I didn't mind.

Huiyi: When I first Nemish's picture to my mom, she said, 'I don't care what culture or country he comes from. If he is a good guy, and you like each other, then just go for it.' But then she said, 'Don't tell your dad yet.' I only told dad after mom had had a 'prep' talk with him.

Nemish was yet to tell his parents about me. I would ask Nemish daily, 'Have you told your parents?' He would say, 'No, not today. Not yet. Let me find a good moment.' One day, I became upset. Only then he agreed.

Nemish: I told my parents the next day. I had felt challenged. I had only known her for two and a half months. Though my parents were open-minded, their world was still conservative. They were also travelling then, their first trip outside India, to my brother's place in the US. I was with them and hoping to find the most suitable time.

We decided to do things the right way and to tell our parents before committing to a relationship. We didn't want a scenario where we had to fight our parents when we have fully committed to each other already.

That day, I told my parents, 'I need to make a phone call to talk to a girl.' When I said the girl was not Indian, they fell silent. They spoke again after two hours, 'Do you have a photo? Can we see her?' They said she looked cute. Things were okay.

Huiyi: It took only sixty days from the day we met to decide to commit to our relationship. I had never dated anyone before Nemish. Nor had I imagined anything happening so fast.

Nemish: My parent's initial silence was not because she was Chinese but because she was a foreigner, something they hadn't expected. As for Chinese people, neither my family nor I had a strong impression of them. Indeed, Indians don't typically like the Chinese, because of the history and war. And the media always portrayed China negatively, covering stupid little stories from some corner of the country. Interestingly, Huiyi had no idea about this war. She was never taught about it in school. That's probably why.

I have travelled to China for work and to visit her family. China's government does a much better job than the Indian government. Every country has its flaws. I don't support everything their government does, but I also believe that if you have a billion people, democracy just doesn't work.

Huiyi: He is more like a Chinese than I am. I don't care much about politics. My dad cares about it a lot. He believes whatever he watches or reads in Chinese media. I tell him, 'Dad, come to Canada, look at things from another perspective, and maybe you will have some new opinions.'

I had never met an Indian until I went to Singapore for my master's degree. In university, I watched Amir Khan movies like the *3 Idiots*. Right before I met Nemish, I was watching *The Newsroom*. Dev Patel (who acted in *The Newsroom*) became my fantasy. He was this stereotypical Indian IT[11] guy, with not much charisma. But he was smart, handsome, and willing to stand up for himself. I told Nemish that he looked like Dev Patel!

In multicultural Singapore, mixed-race couples don't stand out much. Nobody said anything bad to us either. However, there are biases against Indians from India and Chinese from China. My first landlord, a Singaporean–Chinese woman, kept asking, 'Do you have oranges in China? Do you have this? Do you have that?' I could feel her sense of superiority over people like me. But I also had good friends among Singaporean–Chinese colleagues.

Once, two of my Singaporean colleagues went to India on a business trip. Once back, they kept talking about people peeing in the streets, the dust, and how they had diarrhoea. This continued for days and only stopped after they saw me walking with Nemish as a couple. Another colleague complained a lot about her supervisor, an Indian from India. She said Indian people are this, that, blah blah blah. I still feel bad about such stereotyping. Different Indians were treated differently. The locals were more biased against the ones who came from southern India; they were darker and did menial jobs.

Nemish: Some Singaporean–Chinese are racist towards Indians from India. At parties or company events, I never felt welcomed. Compared to Singaporeans, I made more friends with other foreigners.

Huiyi: People in my hometown have a bad impression of Indians. This could be because of Chinese social media—such as Weibo—which is full of negative things about India. People talked only about the crowds, the dirtiness, and caste matters.

---

[11] Information Technology.

Once, an acquaintance asked, 'He must be a Brahmin, right? Otherwise, why would you choose an Indian like him?' 'Oh, he is a vegetarian, then he must be a Brahmin.' They also shared news articles with me, 'Have you ever read this news about Indians? If you marry an Indian, you must look up to your husband, do all the house chores, and then . . . sometimes they will abuse you.'

In Nemish's family, I saw none of these stereotypes. His mom and dad supported each other. If his mom cooked, his dad would chop vegetables and work the dough. His dad also cooked. But maybe his family was not typical. Once, we had a big party in Nemish's apartment. After dinner, instinctively, all the Indian boys just went back to the couch to relax while their Indian girlfriends began cleaning up. I was shocked. We created this mess together. Then, why shouldn't we clean together?

Even on our wedding day, one relative asked my parents, 'How could you let your one and only daughter marry an Indian and go to India?' They gave an 'I feel sorry for you' look even when my parents explained that we were going back to Singapore, not India.

But nowadays, my relatives post good things about India on social media. Maybe this is because of us. My uncle recently shared this article about Rishi Sunak becoming the prime minister of the UK. Another uncle commented, 'Indians are really smart.' And when they read something bad about India, they check with my mom if it's true.

Nemish: My parents visited China for the first time when we held the Chinese wedding there. They were very impressed with their infrastructure. They couldn't believe that even Huiyi's small city had such highways, high-rise buildings, and malls.

Huiyi: My parents, though, were very stressed about arranging this wedding. They rented an apartment, so Nemish's parents could cook there. His mom brought along Indian spices. His parents even cooked for my parents once. But I could tell from my parents' reaction, that they were being polite when trying the food. For our wedding reception, the hotel prepared a full table of vegetarian dishes. But Nemish's parents didn't touch them at all.

Nemish: It was for a simple reason—the hotel made the food look like meat. There was no meat, but it looked like it, my parents just couldn't make themselves eat it.

I liked the Chinese wedding. I liked how the grandparents and parents were invited to give speeches. When my dad gave my mom credit for raising us kids well, her family and relatives were impressed, 'Wait, the husband acknowledged the wife on stage in front of everyone.' They hadn't imagined this.

Huiyi: I love that memory. My parents and grandma's speeches were too formal. But his dad's speech was touching, full of emotions. He said that I was an angel coming to their family and that they would treat me like a daughter. I still remember all of it.

Our wedding in China was modest. Only close friends and family were invited. My mom worked in the government, so we were not allowed to invite more than ninety-nine people. I wore a white gown, he wore a suit. We walked down the aisle, exchanged vows, and gave speeches. And that was it.

Our Indian wedding was also very compressed. We just had the priest, the fire, and some religious things. Within a few hours, it was over. Yet, it was more stressful than our Chinese wedding.

Nemish: Left to us, we would have chosen a very simple wedding. But to satisfy our parents, we ended up spending two and a half weeks getting married. There were two cultures, and two cities. My parents sponsored the Indian wedding. Her parents sponsored the Chinese one. We did all the flights and hotels. There was never any question about dowry.

My parents planned a small Indian wedding. And when I say small, it means only 300 people were invited. But 500 people turned out. Because everyone was so excited to meet her.

Huiyi: I didn't know any of them. They got on stage, took a picture with me, and then got off. Wearing a heavy Indian wedding dress and a fake wig, I stood on stage like a human-size cardboard. This went on for three hours. I was having a fever that night. I felt drowsy. I just stood there, motionless. It was intense. But it was also interesting.

I loved the ceremonies. In one game, the bride and the groom had to fight to grab a key from inside a clay pot. The winner is likely to take charge of the family. Nemish got the key first but then passed it to me secretly. I thought my mother-in-law would like her son to win, but she enjoyed the game.

Once, his auntie tapped my shoulder, asking me to sit down. But everyone else was standing. So I said, 'No, I don't want to sit down.' This made everyone very happy. It turned out that it was a test. Will the new bride sit down without asking her husband first?

Nemish: Her parents, too, flew to Chennai for the wedding. They enjoyed the architecture of the temples and the seafood. But overall, their reaction to Chennai was mixed. They had expected more high-rise buildings in one of India's biggest cities.

Huiyi: I took my parents sightseeing in Chennai. They were so excited when they saw cows on the highway, just like they had heard about India. I said, 'Okay, this has now come true.' I knew it was rare, but unfortunately, it happened.

Nemish: We had many conflicts and quarrels in the first year of our marriage. Sometimes, she might say the wrong words because of her limited English vocabulary. I would then get mad. And sometimes, she wouldn't understand what I was saying. These conflicts were perhaps necessary. Through them, we learnt how to communicate, compromise, and find common ground.

Huiyi: Food and language are our main challenges. Religion has never been one. I join his parents for *puja* (Indian prayers). My non-religious parents don't mind. All religions try to achieve the same anyway: be good and treat others well. And I'm still very curious about Indian culture. While we were dating, I watched many documentaries about India. Here in Canada, I teach Indian culture to grade-three students.

Even today, food is my biggest concern. When we are with his parents, I can eat most dishes they cook. But I can't force myself to eat some dishes, especially fermented ones like idli. His mom tries very hard to make different items for me, but when I can't eat something, I just can't.

It was very hard for Nemish when he first went with me to China. My parents also found it hard to find food for him. We Hakkas have a meat-based cuisine. The only vegetarian dishes are fried eggs with tomato, fried potato, and fried greens. These are not very nutritious.

Moreover, if we have kids someday, his parents may not want them to be eating meat. My parents won't like our kids going vegetarian. When my dad heard of Nemish, his first question was, 'Are you sure? He is a vegetarian. You have to give it a second thought.' He is still worried about me becoming a vegetarian. Whenever I call him, he insists, 'You can't be a vegetarian, okay? Your body is used to meat. Becoming a vegetarian is not good for you. You must eat meat.'

I hope to influence my father through my mother. She is more open-minded.

I miss Singapore for its food court culture. Everyone there can share the same table while eating different food. But here in Canada, where we live now, eating together has become challenging. I can eat vegetarian for up to two days at a stretch. Any longer, I'd feel weak. I crave some meat. We cook most days, and that makes it even harder.

Nemish: On my first trip to China, I had to eat things I wasn't used to for all three meals of the day. But we got through it. Our trips to India and China helped us understand each other and paved our way to marriage. They have made us better prepared. Now, I can not only eat eggs but even century eggs. I like Chinese food now because it is milder. My Indian cooking, too, has become much milder. Now, I cook meat too, only for her because I won't eat it. Sometimes I cook something up to a point, then take my portion out, and then add meat for her. Huiyi cooks meat at home. I have gotten used to the smell. But my parents are not. So she doesn't fry meat at home when they stay with us.

I don't care if my kids are not vegetarians. It is not easy being a vegetarian. I struggle to find vegetarian food on my business trips.

Huiyi: Regarding language, his parents speak English for basic communication but prefer Tamil if they want to say something more complex. I don't speak Tamil at all.

My parents don't speak any English. Sometimes I get stressed about all the communication challenges. To make my dad happy, I pushed Nemish to learn some Mandarin. But if I push too much, he will bounce back. That's when we quarrel.

My first language is not Mandarin, it's Hakka. There's a famous saying: 'Hakkas would rather sell their ancestral land than forget their language.' But I would choose to speak Mandarin with my kids, not Hakka. How will my parents feel about that?

We left Singapore out of concern for our future kids. We do not agree with Singapore's PSLE[12] system, where someone's future is decided when they are just twelve. Both of us grew up in a very competitive environment. We don't want the same for our kids. We want our kids to be all-rounded and not just be judged based on academic performance.

After we left Singapore, we first moved to Toronto. It is a city of immigrants. People there are open-minded. We loved it a lot. But then we had to move to Calgary, a more conservative place. Here, even if no one discriminates openly, the general attitude to minorities is not very welcoming. But migration here is increasing. Hopefully, by the time our kids are born, Calgary will become more multicultural.

Nemish: We are not very 'minority' here. The Chinese population here is big enough to have a consulate. And Indians are very well-respected in Canada. An Indian leads the third biggest political party here. During Covid, some people said, 'I don't like Asians,' or 'I don't want you to be in my city.'

---

[12] Primary School Leaving Examination, a national examination in Singapore held at the end of six years of primary schooling.

But things have been better since last year (2021). It will change more in the coming years.

Raising a family in Canada means there will be cultural compromises. By default, my kids will be bilingual, in French and English. I don't mind if they don't speak Tamil, my mother tongue. Unlike Mandarin, Tamil is not an international language. There's no benefit in learning it. My parents can communicate with them in English.

I am more concerned with the kids' identity. I heard people from mixed families struggle with identity. Am I Chinese, Indian, or Canadian? These questions can be hard. We must train our kids to be confident with their identities.

Huiyi: I don't have a concern about identity. Having studied and lived in various countries, I am multi-identity. Do I think of Canada as home? To me, home is where my parents are. I am an only child. When they are old, they need to stay with me. But I am confident I can raise my kids to accept their mixed-identity too. My biggest concern is whether we get to raise the kids our own respective way, I mean vegetarian or non-vegetarian.

V

The allure of an exotic culture often entices people, making them vulnerable in the process. Are these choices driven by impulsivity? While the initial connection may feel like a match made in heaven, the reality sets in as the couple descends to earth and deals with the aftermaths of their own decisions.

In an interracial relationship, is it possible for one to fully assimilate into their partner's culture? Some individuals in Chinese–Indian relationships may find themselves drawn by the spiritual allure of India or the economic opportunities in China, leading them to attempt such adaptation. But can this adaptation truly override one's own cultural background? And can culture also become a convenient excuse?

Let's Meet in Nepal

Story of Chen Chunyan, thirties, Chinese, and Vikramaditya Myadi, thirties, Indian. They are married and staying in Nepal, awaiting Chen's spouse visa for India.

Vikramaditya: I was named after Vikramaditya, the legendary king. This was because I had big hands, nose, neck, shoulders and teeth. Moreover, I was born on a special day, the day of Diwali, our biggest festival.

I couldn't walk even when I was two years old. But my grandmother said, 'He is Vikramaditya, so don't worry. He will not just walk but do great things in life.' Soon I started walking.

I grew up in a small village called Sadra in the western state of Gujarat in India. My parents were illiterate. We were always very poor. I failed school in my very first year. My aunt gave me a severe beating for this. So I promised myself that I would never fail in my life again. I started working hard. From then onwards, I always came first in school. I also did well in painting, music, games, and yoga.

I did my bachelor's in commerce, but after that did my masters in yoga. During college, I began working part-time as a labourer.

I met Chen on 5 March 2020. There was a yoga festival in Rishikesh[13]. I was working there as a yoga teacher and translator. It was 10 a.m. The sun was shining bright. I was alone, practising yoga. I noticed her walking along with another yoga master. I could sense that she wanted to talk to me, but the man prevented her. She walked far away, and from there, she took my picture. Then she jumped over a railing, came running to me, and asked, 'Hello, how are you?' Our story had begun.

We exchanged numbers, and then we met again on 8 March. We roamed around Rishikesh. I heard people saying, 'Corona, Corona' (an insult to her being Chinese). So I asked her to change into Indian clothes. Then we went to Babadham temple. There, I proposed to her.

You may say all this happened too fast. Well, I am a face-reading master. I could read her fully. And I have learnt yoga for twenty years, so I have a strong touching–feeling sense. Just by touching someone, I can tell their character. And there is a time for everything. Take what you have today because tomorrow, the same thing won't be yours.

Chen Chunyan: I come from the province of Shanxi in China. As a child, I saw my mom always crying, because her in-laws didn't like her.

I have been very independent since a young age. I always topped my class. In school, I was assigned various leadership roles. Then my dad had a car accident, and my family couldn't afford my school fees. I was in grade three of middle school then.

I was taken out of school for one and a half years. When I started studying again, I couldn't do very well. I only managed to get into a junior college to study computers.

---

[13] City in northern India, known as the yoga capital of the world.

After graduation, I opened a clothing store in a shopping mall. I could break even in the first two months, but the shopping mall cheated everyone and closed down without paying back our deposit.

I moved to Taiyuan, the capital of Shanxi. There, I came across *Yoga Sutra*[14]. There are three thick volumes, but I studied them carefully, word by word. It made me calm. I learned about self-containment and gratitude.

Inspired by *Yoga Sutra*, I decided to visit India and learn more about yoga. In 2018, I signed up for an organized tour of India. But the organizer became pregnant and cancelled the tour. I decided to go by myself. I bought the flight tickets even though the prices had risen from ¥2,000 to ¥5,000 by then. It was my first flight and my first time going overseas.

I was told that India is dirty, messy, and dangerous. But I believe that there is always something good in every place, just that people don't talk about them on the internet. However, I was very scared upon reaching Delhi. I saw so many people, so many cars, and so many police with guns. I saw big contrasts: slums next to beautiful houses. At road junctions, I saw people in white performing mysterious rituals. Guns, religion, poverty. Everything seemed to be broken.

I panicked all through the ten-hour bus ride to Rishikesh. Everyone else was sleeping. But what if my bus was hijacked? But once we reached Rishikesh, I could feel the special energy of the place. It was 1 a.m., but the Ganges, the stars, and the moon over Rishikesh calmed me down. I was no longer scared and wondered why I'd even felt so.

My yoga school was basic, but everyone greeted me with a 'namaste'. I recalled my purpose, to find and experience yoga.

---

[14] The *Yoga Sutras of Patañjali* are an ancient collection of Sanskrit sutras (aphorisms) on the theory and practice of yoga.

We went to the Himalayan caves to meditate. Sitting inside, I could hear my blood flowing inside me. There was no need to chant 'Om . . .', my body and the universe worked naturally to produce the sound of 'Om . . .'

Once, while meditating, I lost myself and saw a light dawning on me. I was so scared that I stopped meditating ever since. I told my guru about this strange experience. He said that I had opened my third eye. I had unlocked my throat chakra. From being a person of few words, I became talkative.

In 2020, I opened a yoga studio in China. I had planned to take my students to India for the International Yoga Festival at Rishikesh. Just then, Covid began. My students couldn't go, but I went alone.

That morning, I developed an uncomfortable stomach when outside. I was walking back to my hotel, and then I saw him practising yoga. He was bathed in the morning sunlight. His pose was perfect. He looked so elegant, his toned body so beautiful. He was so handsome in his traditional Indian scarf. Despite all the people around him, he practised yoga with such serenity as if he was all alone in this world and nothing else mattered. I took photos and videos of him, from afar because I didn't want to disturb him. When I was about to leave, I heard him calling, 'Come, come.' There was a two-metre high fence between us, but I jumped over it.

He was the first person I added on WhatsApp. Another yoga teacher tried to deter me from him, asking me to be careful. Indian yoga teachers are infamous in China for the sex scandals with their female students. Some, who had married Chinese girls, were later found to have hidden the fact that they were already married to someone in India. As such, I was cautious with Indian yoga teachers. So when Vikram called me multiple times, I chose not to answer. Then a Chinese yoga teacher, who was also there in Rishikesh, told me that Vikram was a good person. Only then, I answered his call.

We went around Rishikesh together. He took me to pay respect at a master's tomb. We sat along the banks of the Ganges, talking about yoga. Then came the festival of Holi, when Indians throw colours at each other. My ticket back to China was waiting for me. But I went out with him. I already liked him by then. On the day of Holi, he held my hands. Some yogis saw us and asked about him about me. He said that I was his girlfriend. When some colour got into my nose, he brought out his handkerchief and twisted it into a cone to clean my nose with its tip. I was shocked. It was such a clean handkerchief, but he didn't mind. He was so caring. I felt my body as accepted.

The next day, he proposed marriage. I was not surprised. I said yes. That day, we didn't feel like leaving each other. For a long time, we just sat on the road together.

Vikramaditya: I told my sister about Chen and that we wanted to get married. She said, go ahead. We wanted to get married right away, in a temple. But Chen was having her period then, so we couldn't. Also, she had no 'single certificate'.

In between, I took her to our home to introduce her to my family and relatives. Because of Corona, there was a lot of anti-Chinese feeling in India. My relatives, my fellow villagers, everyone was going against me because of this. My family was against our marriage not just because of the pandemic. In India, caste is such a big thing. They worried that she was from a low caste. Moreover, in India, people think that the Chinese eat dogs and all kinds of things. That was an issue too. I told them that she is vegetarian, and that is final. I said that I didn't know about anyone else, but I trusted her.

Because we couldn't proceed further, I asked Chen to return to China to get the documents and come back by May because May is the wedding season. But she didn't want to go back. She feared that there would be a big lockdown and she wouldn't be able to return to India. I had not anticipated the lockdown situation to become that bad. So she left for China.

It took almost one and a half years to get my parent's approval for our marriage. It was a big struggle. Chen doesn't know what I was actually going through. Only my heart knows how I worked hard to win their support. But I always told her, 'You don't worry. If I have to leave my society, my village, and my family, for you, I will still do it for you.'

As for Chen's parents, I have only spoken to them twice, over video. There is no need to talk much if the people who matter trust each other. And sometimes, the more you talk, the worse the situation becomes. So it is more important to act.

Chen Chunyan: Once back in China, I informed my parents of my decision to marry Vikram. My mom had heard of bad stories where girls involved with foreign men couldn't return to China because their IDs were seized (by the man). I told her, 'Mom, that story was in Africa. Also, on Kuaishou and TikTok,[15] people only talk about bad things.' My parents also wished for me to stay near them. As such, they didn't support our marriage. But only I could decide my relationship. They had no choice but to accept it.

Vikramaditya: Two days after Chen left for China, India declared a complete lockdown. Things got even worse when India and China started to fight a war. In hindsight, we made the right decision. Her visa would have expired otherwise.

---

[15] Kuaishou and TikTok are two of the top social media platforms in China.

There was no way I could support her also because I soon lost my job because of the lockdown.

Chen Chunyan: We had only eight days together in India. And then, we were separated for 700 days. We stayed in touch only through online chat. I don't like to do video calls, so we talked mostly through texting. This would make him suspect that I was seeing someone else. We fought a lot then. But I told him, 'Wait for me if you want, but anyway, I'll come to India to marry you.'

I never doubted my decision to marry him. He is a hardworking and persistent person. He is persistent about his work, studies, and his love for me. Without missing a single day, he said 'good morning' and 'good evening' to me. I believed that he would wait for me. But because we couldn't meet, I often became moody and made things difficult for him. He tolerated my bad tempers.

One day, he said, 'Let's meet in Nepal.'

Vikramaditya: It was a really tough time. Because of the war, India banned TikTok and WeChat. I tried many things, but there was no way for us to stay in touch. Because of the war, her parents turned against our relationship also. And because of all these things that were happening, Chen stopped talking to me as well. And all this while, I didn't even have enough money to eat. But I stayed strong.

I finally managed to contact Chen on DingTalk. One of my students who knew her got us connected again. Slowly, we started from where we had left off. I told Chen, 'Don't you worry. Times are tough, but I am here waiting for you.'

After a few months, I went to Baroda to study ayurveda. I also began working as a therapist and yoga instructor. Then we both came to Nepal to get married.

I explored many options for us to get married. I looked at Hong Kong, I looked at Sri Lanka. Nepal was the most attractive. We could get the 'single certificate' there and at decent costs. And Chen could get a spouse visa for India from Nepal if we married there. So I contacted a top legal service in Nepal that arranged such foreigner-weddings. I paid them an advance, and we got our 'single certificates'.

It wasn't easy to get the 'single certificate'. Even the marriage officers said, 'She is Chinese. Why are you taking such risks?' Around that time, many Chinese were getting arrested in India. But I didn't budge. I made such people shut up. I told such people on the face that many things that are portrayed as true aren't true, that mass media will say anything to sell a story, and that people will say anything, blame anyone, to become famous.

As Kabir has said, 'I went to find evil in the whole world, and I couldn't find it anywhere, then I looked inside myself, and the evil was sitting right there.' People are what they are because of their circumstances. No human wants to do anything evil. It is their circumstances that make them do certain things. And people change with time. So, we shouldn't blame anyone. If we point one finger at others, three fingers will point back at us. So first and foremost, we should trust our own feelings. We should then make decisions based on our own feelings, not on other people's thinking. If I feel right with her, I should marry her. Our own experience should be our guide. Experience gives us the best knowledge of our world. We just need to have the courage and move ahead.

We have only had a legal wedding so far. For that day, I got her dressed in Indian clothes. But we will do a proper ceremony and reception in India someday. We have to give her a party, right? We have to get her to know my people. And we have to let my people know her.

Chen Chunyan: He introduces me to all his friends, saying this is my wife, my wife, my wife. But I have not officially announced our relationship to my friends yet. Everyone, however, can see my WeChat portrait, which shows us together. Some comment that Indian food seems unpalatable just judging by the look. I told them it's the same for Chinese food. Some Chinese food looks good, and some does not. Some comment that now they are learning more about Indian culture. But they all agree that Vikram looks good.

Vikramaditya: I like many things about the Chinese—their style of working, and their quick decision-making. In fact, I agree with the Communist Party of China. At least they can make decisions and get things moving. Unlike our country where Modiji is trying hard to develop India, but people keep pulling his leg.

I am not worried about things happening to us because of anti-Chinese sentiments in India. The more you fear things, the less you can live. She is sometimes afraid. But she doesn't need to be. Everyone knows I am married to a Chinese girl. I post on Facebook. No one has passed any negative comments. She can pass off as a Nepali or Tibetan if she wears their kind of clothes. And with a certain kind of make-up, she can even pass for an Indian.

And I don't care about our language differences. I work with humanity. When you work with humanity, language doesn't matter. Anyway, she is learning some Gujarati. I have also learnt some Chinese.

Chen Chunyan: Even if I don't say anything, he understands me with one glance. We have telepathy.

Anyway, I bought him Chinese language textbooks from the Confucius school—levels one to four. Vikram has this dream of living with my parents in their village, cooking, eating, and chatting with them every day. When he and my parents had their first video call, he was dancing. He wants to blend into my life completely—my parents, my family, and my friends. He also wants me to integrate into his life, friends, and family. His family likes me as well. They even made Chinese noodles for me.

Vikramaditya: But one thing I find difficult about the Chinese is that they are very stubborn. And she gets angry with me sometimes.

Chen Chunyan: Perhaps it's their culture, he has a lot of friends. His phone calls are nonstop. He can talk for hours on the phone with another person, man or woman, old or young . . . And then, there is Trisha. Vikram met her only in August. But they keep calling each other, texting, video calling, more than ten times a day, from morning until night, every day, sometimes at 1 a.m., 3 a.m., 4 a.m. They talk more than Vikram and I do.

To be fair, this Trisha often talks about me and asks Vikram to be nice to me. Once, Vikram and I had problems and stopped talking to each other. He even gave up processing the 'single certificate'. Back then, Trisha urged him to marry me. But I don't care what they talk about. I am angry that they talk way too much. I don't know if it's in Indian culture for women and men to talk so much to each other. But good friends also must contain themselves. Imagine, she calls herself Radha, him Krishna. I don't like this Radha–Krishna analogy—it's for people in love.

Vikramaditya: Trisha is my best friend. Her family knows me, her kids know me. And in Gujarat, we can be very friendly with friends. Men and women can joke freely. But Chunyan always thinks too much. Because of her doubts, I have lost over 100 friends. The way we Indians take every relationship to our hearts—they (the Chinese) don't take it the same way.

Chen Chunyan: Then there is the question of having kids. He doesn't want kids. But I want two, three, five . . . the more, the merrier. Children should be part of life. And it's intriguing to have a mixed child. But he thinks the kids will trap us. Well, I am also okay with not having kids, especially looking at how some kids treat their old parents.

But I want to have at least one child. I am thirty-six. He is six years younger than me. Perhaps he doesn't want kids because he is young . . .

Vikramaditya: I don't care for kids much. I don't want kids if that takes away our love and respect. The next generation will be too digital, with no emotions. Only devices, and just transactional relationships. There will be no heart. Kids will ask too much of parents—money, all that. There will be too many quarrels between kids and parents. I know all this. But she doesn't know. Yet, it is not in our hands whether we will have children. God and fate will decide it.

Chen Chunyan: We have always needed patience and perseverance, whether we were together or apart. We have been through a lot. But we have always needed to trust and believe in each other. To me, his perseverance and trust were a manifestation of Indian culture.

We plan to shuttle between India and China. We'll also go to other countries. We will study. I want to learn ayurveda. We plan to open a studio in China, for yoga and wellness. We will travel around in villages as ayurvedic doctors, solving conditions like insomnia or headaches. But we will be centred around life, not work.

Everywhere in the world is the same. People are the same. There is good and bad everywhere, among all people. But overall, I like Indian culture, and I like him.

Vikramaditya: I have told her, 'You set the goals. I will set the path.'

But I have only one thing to say, that respect is more important than love. You can find love easily, but it is not easy to find respect. I respect her. And I will respect her all my life. Because I am an Indian. And one thing I will respect is if she decides to leave me someday. I told Chen, 'I love you, so you stay as my partner for as long as you wish. If you want to leave me one day, please do. But even then, I will always be waiting for you. I know you will come back. I know you won't be able to live anywhere without me.' Love shouldn't become like bondage. Love should set you free. So I want her to be free. I am here to take care of her. I am not here to bind her. I am not here to make her sad.

Yet, I know she can't find anyone like me. I believe in myself. But I have also told her, 'You can take away everything from me. But don't take away my friends.' Lovers shouldn't spoil lives.

No one will struggle for her as much as I did. I have fought so many things for her. I fought casteism, religion and all that. I have left so many opportunities for her. One rich girl invited me to Thailand to get married to her. But I will not be bought. Because I am a Gujarati.

Once Our Vibrations Matched, Nothing Else Mattered

Story of Xiaoqing (Kamala), thirties, Chinese, and Girish, thirties, Indian. They are married and live in India.

Kamala: I grew up in a big extended family. In our small town in Jiangsu, China, we were considered rich. My maternal grandma had twelve children. Nine of them survived. Each had one factory. And yet, there were always money-related disputes among the siblings. I sometimes heard my uncles complaining about one another. I was shocked. Why are we unhappy when we are so wealthy? Is there no path to inner peace regardless of wealth? I kept having these thoughts, which, over time, directed me towards a spiritual journey. This is how I got to know my husband.

Girish: I come from a middle-class family in Bangalore, India. We are a family of engineers. I am also a part-time Hindustani classical musician. Since a young age, I have followed Sahaja Yoga[16]. I met Xiaoqing through a match by Sahaja Yoga. We dated through phone calls for one and a half months. Then she came to India to marry me.

---

[16] A religious sect that emphasizes meditation.

Kamala: I learned about Sahaja Yoga while I was studying in Shanghai. I was touched by the love, warmth, and wisdom of our teacher. I developed a deep faith in her. Rarely did I trust anyone this way. I was this thirsty person who had finally found the cherished spring. Once I tasted its precious water, I could never let it go. I wanted my other half also to be a Sahaja Yogi. Or else, what if he couldn't recognize its value? That would be a big shame.

I had heard of other Chinese yogis who had gotten into happy marriages through Sahaja Yoga. So I filled up their application form for matchmaking. The form was first sent to our leader for eastern China, then to our country leader, and all our applications were then aggregated in Italy. The matching committee there chose matches depending on the individuals' vibrations. They email the matched parties who can then contact each other and decide the next steps.

When I was told about my match with a practitioner from India, I didn't think at all about the country, his age, profession, or family background. My only thought was, is his faith in the teacher as deep as mine?

Girish: The application form had the option of being open to foreigners. I had ticked yes. Many of my school friends had foreign spouses. And, after all, the purpose of such a matching process was to let the world become one.

After submitting my application, I had somehow forgotten about it altogether. I just continued with life as usual. Then one fine day, they sent me a live-streaming link. When I opened it, I heard my name being called. My ear perked up. It said I was matched with a girl from China. I had difficulty registering her name. So, I played back the recording of that live-streaming four or five times to note it down. I texted one of my yogi friends who practised in China, asking if he knew this girl. He gave me her number. I had full faith in Sahaja Yoga's style of matching people by vibrations. So I contacted Xiaoqing even before the committee arranged for us to know each other.

Xiaoqing was the first real Chinese person I came to know. Before that, I had only seen Chinese people in movies. But I felt like I had known her for many years from the moment we first connected. So I closed my eyes and surrendered completely to her. She, too, felt the same way. By the time the official email came, we already liked each other. Our relationship was like a high-speed train. We had complete trust in each other. Imagine, she left home to marry someone she had only spoken to over the phone, that too in a strange country.

Kamala: I decided to marry Girish as soon as I was convinced that Girish was a faithful practitioner. Within a month and a half of our first call, I had already booked my tickets to India. I had just a week before the trip, and I hadn't yet found the courage to tell my parents. My mum is a strong woman, a high achiever. She was proud of me because I was the first to obtain a postgraduate degree within my extended family. Would she break down hearing my decision? After all, outsiders can hardly appreciate Sahaja Yoga fully.

Girish insisted that I must inform my family. If I couldn't, we would have to postpone our wedding. With his continuous encouragement, I called my mom. I said, 'I am going to India to marry an Indian.' Then I just hung up. I couldn't face her meltdown.

I kept my phone switched off until the next day. About lunchtime, I called my younger sister, who said it would be okay to call my mom again. As expected, mom had had a massive meltdown. She scolded everybody she could find, as she couldn't get to me. My father told her, 'You need to be clear that Xiaoqing is only informing us, not asking for our advice.

You must accept it whether you want to or not.' Mom calmed down after that.

Girish: When she told me she hung up on her mom, I thought, 'Oh my god, this will be a roadblock.' But just within a few days, things became smooth. It shows her family's simplicity and their trust in each other.

Kamala: Since a young age, my parents have always given me full freedom. They had full faith in my decisions. Even when we thought differently, they believed I had my reasons. Yet, it was a miracle to get my parents' acceptance so fast.

My mom loves the Chinese song, 'Only Mother Is Good in the World.' As Girish can sing, I made him sing this song to her. My mother cried hearing him sing. At that moment, she accepted Girish fully.

Girish: There was silence on the other end when I sang that song. But I could hear her crying. I wasn't sure if it was my lousy singing or . . . [laughs].

Kamala: I flew to India alone, with my two luggage bags. Girish received me at Delhi airport. Three days later, we got married in Jaipur. We were part of a mass wedding organized by Sahaja Yoga. There were sixty couples, including us. Sahaja Yoga arranged everything, all we needed to do was to follow instructions.

I was moved by the traditional ritual of *havan*. We walked seven rounds around the fire altar. A long white cloth divided the bride and bridegroom. We chanted together. With each chant, we took one step towards each other. People around blessed us, throwing rice into the air.

Girish: After our wedding, we visited Xiaoqing's hometown in China. There I met her extended family for the first time. Everyone accepted me and our marriage. Though I come from a vegetarian family, I do eat meat. So I was able to enjoy Chinese food. This made them happy. 'This Indian can eat everything!' They were pleasantly surprised I knew their factory machines. I am an engineer in industrial manufacturing, after all.

Her hometown is a small county. People there do not know much about the world. So I heard stereotypes like 'Indians have dark skin,' and 'all Indians do IT.' But generally, they were very polite. There were more similarities than differences between us. Indians and Chinese share many common values, such as how we care for the elderly and connect to extended families. This 'big family' concept is dying in India, but I found it still alive in her hometown. The only culture shock was the excessive smoking and drinking. I, on the other hand, have never smoked or drunk alcohol. This led to funny situations. One day, her cousin—who had become close to me—offered me a cigarette. He was so shocked when I refused. Everyone else was surprised too. They discussed extensively if it was for health or religious reasons.

Kamala: After this trip, I settled down with his family in India. The biggest culture shock for me was the food. I just couldn't get used to Indian food. Moreover, my mother-in-law—who cooked for all of us—only made vegetarian dishes as they were strict vegetarians. So my first three years in India were very difficult. Of course, I missed my family. But I also missed Chinese food a lot. I often went starving because I would rather not eat Indian food. When my parents visited India for a few days, they, too, found Indian food very difficult to get used to. It just tastes too different from Chinese food.

Now we have separate kitchens, and I cook my own food. I can cook meat. Everyone else in the house also likes my Chinese cooking, except my mom-in-law—she cannot eat my meat dishes.

But I could endure all such difficulties because I loved my life in India. I had been to India a few times, even before our wedding. And every time, it felt very natural. I could immediately blend into the environment. When I first came to Mumbai, I was taken aback by the dirtiness and messiness. I was shocked to see men peeing freely in the streets. But then, I would miss Mumbai immediately upon returning to Shanghai, as if Mumbai was my hometown.

I integrated into his family very quickly. My parents-in-law are both faithful practitioners of Sahaja Yoga. I love talking with them about their insights. Their wisdom nourishes me. Girish, too, is both a teacher and a friend. All these years, he has helped me immensely in my spiritual growth. I can talk to him about anything in the world. Even if I wake him up past midnight, he agrees to talk. Living with him, I don't need friends.

In India, I worked in a law firm for a while but became a full-time housewife after we had our two girls. In my childhood, I was deprived of time with my mom. She was always busy. Even at the dining table, she could not pay attention to us. Her mind was always on her factory and employees. My mother-in-law and husband think highly of a mother's role. They say the mother is the family's anchor. A homemaker mother can accompany her children at home and make them feel secure. I agree with this point of view. Yet, I am doing a start-up now, but in a 'zen' mode, promoting a herbal essence brand in China.

Girish: Traditionally, Indian girls are expected to respect elders. They are expected to bring everyone in the family together. Xiaoqing does better than most Indian girls in these aspects. She is very homely. Wherever she goes, she only brings warmth. She even bought gifts for my grandma and uncles, even the ones she was yet to meet. They were all very touched.

It's funny that my relatives were initially doubtful of Xiaoqing. Coming from an orthodox Brahmin community, my parents' involvement in Sahaja Yoga was already a big no for them. My marrying a foreigner was taking a step further. But I told them, 'You will take back your words once you get to know her.' And that is exactly what happened. All my uncles now say that she is better than an Indian girl and that we couldn't have asked for more. The only barrier between them is that Xiaoqing can't speak Tamil. This is, however, not an issue with my parents, because, in our house, we mostly speak English.

But Xiaoqing speaks Chinese when she is very angry [laughs]. She used to get mad at me at times. I couldn't understand why. Then I realized that she had expectations of me. All my life, nobody expected anything from me. I had no expectations of others either. I used to be a worry-free bachelor hanging out with my friends. I was 'lost' on weekends. When my mom asked, 'What time will you come home?' I would reply, 'I don't know.' And mom wouldn't worry unless I was getting too late. But this couldn't continue once we got married. Xiaoqing had left her country to come to a completely unfamiliar place. Everything was new to her—language, food, people. She had only me to talk to. And I was the only person who could speak on her behalf to the rest of the world. She depended on me to feel secure and comfortable. So I had to change my lifestyle. I had to meet her expectations. I had to be the one to take her out or help her buy things. If I said I would return at seven, I would have to.

It took me some time to understand this. I have not changed entirely, but I am making a constant effort. I am getting better. But Xiaoqing has also become a lot more independent by now.

Kamala: It took me three years to become more independent. Now I seek help from my mother-in-law sometimes. As e-commerce has become common in India, my reliance on him for shopping has also reduced. Girish has also realized that he was too fluid earlier. For both of us, it is a learning process.

Over time, I learned to deal with my emotions. I have become more mature. I have also realized that my reliance on him creates many hassles for him. I had taken this reliance for granted.

During our first few years together, my mom kept asking me to return to China. According to her, with his skills, Girish could earn a lot more in China. I would get influenced and ask Girish to make such plans. But after I had kids, I understood that my life was mine, not my mom's. Happy with our state of life, my parents also interfere less now.

Our elder daughter is eight years old, and the younger one is five. Our girls join us when we go to the Sahaja Yoga centre. They have children's activities there. They are also learning meditation. Our eldest can speak Chinese; she loves the Chinese characters. But she feels distant from my family. The younger one then gets influenced by her sister. But I am not worried. Kids adjust very quickly. We visited China before Covid. Both blended in well. Our locals knew they were Indian but were very friendly with them.

Girish: Our elder one looks more like Xiaoqing. She likes Chinese food too. The younger one looks more Indian. And she likes Indian food. The kids get some discrimination in school. Some boys shout at our elder girl, 'You are from China!' She replies, 'No, my mother is from China.' And the boys insist, 'You are from China, don't play with us!' Luckily, most of her friends, especially the girls, are nicer to her. They treat her as just another friend.

Kamala: My elder daughter is more introverted and sensitive. Such talk bothers her. The younger one is a strong character and is not bothered by what others say.

My social circle in India is tiny. But we are delighted with the quality of our friend circle. They are our yogi friends. On Sundays, we go to the Sahaja Yoga centre. We meet our friends there. Our yogi friends are all senior executives. Their mindset is mature and very international. They express love for China and Chinese people. I have never experienced discrimination.

I still wish to go back to China someday. It's, after all, where I grew up. I am still a Chinese citizen. I have never considered becoming an Indian. It will be very meaningful to spread Sahaja Yoga in China and let more people learn about it. But I will not plan or push for anything to happen. Our marriage was never planned, but it happened. And it changed our life.

We Are Now One and the Same

Story of Sofia (name changed), thirties, Chinese, and Marc (name changed), forties, Indian. They are married and live in the United States.

Sofia: I am from Wuhan. After Beijing, Wuhan has the most universities in China. But since very young, I have wanted to study somewhere far from home.

My dad was the youngest son of his family. So my parents spent all our holidays taking care of my grandparents. I had no chance to travel outside. Being the only child, I knew I would probably marry someone from Wuhan too so that I could live my whole life near my parents. My university life would then be my only chance to see the outside world.

I went to Shaoxing city in Zhejiang province to study International Economy and Trading. My specialization was in Textiles. That's how and where I met my husband.

Zhejiang had a booming economy driven by small private enterprises, mostly focused on textiles. Textiles made in cities like Yiwu, Shaoxing, Hangzhou, Jiaxing, and Ningbo go out worldwide. Indians came there to trade in large numbers. Many Chinese–Indian couples first met in Zhejiang.

Marc: I was born in Amritsar in Punjab, India. After that, we moved to Haridwar. I did my bachelor's studies in New Delhi.

Growing up, I was always judged and looked down upon. So, I always wanted to get out of India.

Some from my paternal family had settled in Canada, and some from my maternal family had settled in the US. They became Canadian and American. I was an Indian. At any family gathering, I was treated differently. My American and Canadian cousins had food served on the dining table. I would not be seated with them. I ate while holding my plate in my hands.

I studied in public school. My neighbours' kids went to private schools. So they were not allowed to play with me. Later, when I studied in Delhi, I saw how the city kids dressed up and spent on things. I had none of their privileges.

After I completed my degree in fashion design, I found a job in Hong Kong. Hong Kong has a special place in my heart. There, my career took off. I mingled very well with the local society. One day, I wandered into a building called Chungking Mansions. A Pakistani guy named Kashif paid for my food. I tried to pay him back many times, but he never allowed me to spend a penny. This was Hong Kong. They never looked down upon me.

Then my company opened an office in mainland China. Nobody wanted to leave Hong Kong and join this office. Hong Kong, after all, was a glamorous place with beautiful girls. But I took the opportunity and moved to Guangzhou as the company's chief representative. Even in Guangzhou, I lived my Hong Kong lifestyle. Every night, I went to discos and clubs and met new girls.

Then my company wanted to start a new production plant in Shaoxing. Shaoxing was a remote place back then. It only had KFC, not even McDonald's. Again, I raised my hand when everyone else declined. There, I got the idea of building my own business. I had seen the whole production process by now. To go to clubs and pick up girls, or to build a career in an industrial place? The choice was clear.

Had I stayed in India, I would have been an employee forever. The Indian bosses wouldn't allow me to meet customers or suppliers. They keep such things to themselves. In China, the bosses ask us to meet more customers and bring more orders.

The kind of opportunities China has offered is amazing. I witnessed many young staff's journeys from being fresh graduates to becoming multi-millionaires. In China, whether we were drinking, eating, or in the gym, every discussion led to business. Everyone wants to progress in life. They don't care about your skin colour. They are only focused on business.

Sofia: He chanced upon the good times of China's opening up [laughs].

Marc: But what's the culture in India? Even in school, everyone tries to be a goon, a bully. The current right-wing government is polarizing the nation. Twenty-four seven, the TV channels spread hatred toward Muslims, Christians, Sikhs, lower castes, and other minorities. I would never live in India even if anyone gave me thirty million dollars to do so. It's not for me.

Sofia: We have a Bodhisattva in our house.

Marc: But I don't want my kids to grow up in that environment. Till today, the 'untouchables' are still forbidden to take water from the well in some villages. In China, there is no such thing as caste. Of course, China is not perfect. And I'm saying all this not because I hate India. It's our responsibility to say not only the good things.

On my passport, I am Indian. But from my heart, I am Chinese. I went to China at twenty-five and spent two decades there. I eat Chinese food, drink Chinese wine, and watch Chinese movies more than the Chinese do. I hardly watch Indian movies, but I watch every Hong Kong movie. In China,

I never felt that I was not Chinese. Everyone treated me equally. No one discriminated against me. China is a place that valued, nurtured, and brought me to where I am today.

Sofia: I joined his company as a fresh graduate. He was a pioneer there. But we had terrible impressions of each other.

There were five other Indians in the company. They were all friendly to me. But Marc always ignored me. He used to dash into the office carrying a gym bag, do his work, and then dash off. His eyes grew on top of his head (Chinese saying for someone who is very vain). I thought he was arrogant. Maybe he ignored me because I looked ugly to him and because of my bad fashion sense.

Once, Marc asked me to redo some work again and again. I complained to my colleagues in Mandarin. 'The work will never be finished if he keeps doing it this way!' Marc suddenly turned back fiercely, 'This is work! You must complete it!' I was shocked. He was the boss, after all.

He was very popular among girls. He was tall, good-looking, with a good physique from all his hard work in the gym. The cleaning lady in the office told me that Marc was a playboy, that he changed girlfriends all the time. Other girls would always ask me things about him. They wanted to know when he was free and what he liked to eat.

We didn't have a promising start. But random events pulled us together. If not, we would have said bye-bye to each other long ago.

There was this girl who liked him very much. She organized a group trip to Hangzhou with the purpose of 'catching' him without making it too obvious. She invited me as well. Somehow, everyone fell ill before the trip. Someone had food poisoning, someone got injured when skiing, someone was down with a fever. Only the two of us showed up. Because I didn't like this guy, I just wanted to cancel my trip. But he insisted that I go along. He wanted to buy some shoes and needed me to help him bargain. I said okay. He was the boss, and I had to go with him. By the end of that day, I thought the guy was not so bad. He was funny and treated me to some good food. Or maybe he treated me differently because I wore something okay that day [laughs]. I don't know.

Things changed completely once we came back from Hangzhou. We started exchanging messages. We hung out after office hours. Then we started being together. That girl probably hated me.

But soon, the company sent him to Colombia. He had always wanted that role, and it happened just after we got together. So, I always say to him, I'm your lucky star. I bring good things to you.

Dating a colleague is never a good thing. I thought we would stop contacting each other and drift away, given the long distance. There was no WeChat back then, only MSN and QQ, which were much more troublesome.

Marc: But we talked even more after I went to Colombia. We might not have become so close had I not gone to Colombia.

Sofia: If he didn't go to Colombia, maybe we'd start fighting and break up in those early days. Who knows? He spent seven months in Colombia. Once he came back, he came to Wuhan to meet my father. My mother had passed away, so he could only meet my father.

Marc: In Wuhan, she came to pick me up from the airport. Her father was waiting at his home. Once we reached, he grabbed my bag and started walking, even before I could say hello.

Her father was very caring. He rose early the following day. His morning greeting was, 'What breakfast do you want?' Then he bought noodles, dumplings, and so many other foods. I said, 'No, I'm not in a hotel; you don't have to wake up so early.' But he did it every day.

Even today, when we visit Wuhan, he will get up at five and wait for me to get up. Once I'm up, he will tell me, 'Go brush your teeth. I'm going to bring you noodles.' He doesn't let me do anything. When I try to do small housework like cleaning the floor, he'll say, 'No, No, *ni bu guan*' (you don't bother with this).

I didn't do anything special to win his heart. I have only seen in the movies where a nervous boyfriend tries to convince the girl's father. In my case, I just walked in, and everything was served to me.

Sofia: Marc is a very social guy. He meets all the suppliers and customers. He can talk with people from eight to eighty years old. Everyone, including my father, likes him.

But that's not the whole story. My father didn't like it when I first told him I was dating an Indian. He asked me, 'Are you sure he doesn't already have a wife in his country?' He was also saddened that I may not live next to him in Wuhan any more. He lost his sleep for many days.

Then we had a call. I said, 'I respect your opinion. But at least you spend some time with him. If you still don't like him, I will consider it seriously because you are my father. But you cannot write him off only because he is a foreigner. By this logic, I can marry my neighbour any time because we are close. That will be a stupid reason.' My father agreed. And it was all fine once they met.

Whenever we go to Wuhan, my father only thinks about what Marc wants, not me, not our kids.

Marc: We are blessed from both sides. Her father and my parents were both very open-minded and accepting.

Sofia: His experiences in China were all positive. But he enjoys a foreigner's privilege. As a Chinese, I encounter things he doesn't.

Some people passed comments behind our backs, not all friendly. Once in Shaoxing, my father-in-law was visiting us. Many neighbours assumed he was our mixed kids' father. In their minds, Chinese girls always marry rich foreigners who are very old.

As for his parents, the first time I met them, I already wanted to marry into that family and become its member. Our hearts touched each other. His mother spoke little English, but I felt connected with her. Right after she saw me, she said, 'Marry this girl.'

But other people asked his parents to push him to marry an Indian girl. This was because his elder brother had passed away in an accident, and Marc was left as their only child.

Marc: When a neighbour suggested this, my father replied, 'Do you want my son to betray this girl?' He then told me, 'You have brought this girl to our home. Don't bring anyone else. She's the one, the first, and the last.'

My parents are almost eighty years old, but they are very open-minded. They practice their faith, while I am an atheist. But they never imposed their religion on me. They never asked, 'How could you bring this girl home? You are not even married.' They never asked whether she eats beef or whether she wears skirts. They never said I must find a girl from the same religion or state.

Sofia: We have not travelled much in India. When we go home there, he always tells me it is unsafe outside. So we spend all the time just sitting at home. Once, we visited his mother's uncle in Amritsar. It looked less developed than any small town in China. But everyone seemed to be coming out of elite education. Young kids there spoke very good English. Teenagers confidently shared their plans. It felt surreal, given the broken roads and houses around us. In China, married kids move out of their parent's house. But for that family in Amritsar, everyone was living together—all their three sons, their wives, kids, parents.

My biggest challenge in India is not being able to eat meat. Everyone there was vegetarian. After having no meat for one month, I felt like nabbing the chickens roaming the streets.

All this went well, but even after dating for three years, Marc didn't want to get married. He feared marriage, thinking he couldn't be with someone for long. And he didn't want to tell lies. He had like 500 girlfriends before. When our colleagues knew we were dating, they called me the five-zero-one. 501 was my number.

Marc: I was very focused on my career. Those days, I travelled extensively. I was in one city today and in another tomorrow. I could not be bound. Earlier, I would just go to a club and date whomever I met that night. The next day, I would be free and back to my work. I met beautiful girls but knew I wouldn't marry them.

But for marriage, I wanted a family-oriented and responsible girl. I am a wild horse. I want to go all out for my career. So I needed a person to hold me and bind the family together. Sofia was perfect in that regard.

Sofia: I see it differently. Marc cares a lot about his image. He works hard to make money and build his career. This is because he feels insecure deep inside. His ex-girlfriends were either much more beautiful or much more intelligent than me. But once in a relationship, they always wanted to ensure his commitment. This was understandable, especially since he was a foreigner. But then they would start checking his mobile phone, asking whom he had met and when he would marry her. Marc then just wanted to run away. How can an insecure person offer a sense of security and stability to others?

But I am different. My father is a very loving person. Even when my mother was alive, he did all the housework, cooked, and cared for her. So, I always felt safe. I can manage any life situation. We were in the US when I was pregnant with our first baby. The day my water broke, Marc also sprained his back badly. He just could not move. He got so scared. Then I told him, relax, I will handle it. I called a taxi and went to the hospital by myself. I came back home with a baby and his dinner.

I make Marc feel secure. So he always tells me the truth. He has had a colourful life. He never lied that I was the first person he loved. I told him that it was okay, that till we are together, we will enjoy together, and whatever happens in the future, we will see in the future. I will be fine if one day, you want to go back to that life or if you don't love me any longer. I will carry on.

Marc: It is true. While we were well settled in Shaoxing, she once went to Shuqian to meet her friend. Four days later, she returned and said, 'I'm going to live in Shuqian. I'm taking the two kids. I'm taking the two maids.' I said, 'Are you crazy? You just went to meet your friend, and you want to change the city?' She said yes. On she went. I stayed back for a month. Then she sent some photos, 'Look at the gym. Look at the gym.' I joined her in Shuqian. That's how much I trust her.

Sofia: Now, he always says, 'That city was the best.' We lived for three years in Shuqian and have our best memories from there.

I believe a good marriage is not about how deeply you love each other but how you can grow together from strength to strength. If you grow, one can be the other's backbone when they need you. This is how power should be balanced in a relationship. Before Shuqian, we had started a trading business together. But I did nothing there, I was just the boss's wife. Sometimes he also hinted at this when we fought. I hated it. Where was my value? So I went to Shuqian to start a school by myself. Then I hired him as a teacher at my school. I am your boss now, you know?

Then one day, I told him I didn't want to live in China any more. I wanted to go to a foreign country because, in China, he depended on me for everything. Another consideration was our children. People in Shuqian hadn't met many foreigners. They found our kids interesting and were loving. But they stood out. I don't want my kids to be special. Whether this special means good or bad, I prefer them to be normal. I want them to be themselves. So I said, let's move to the US. Here in the US, their school is thirty per cent white, thirty per cent Indian, and the rest are north Asians. I like this diversity where my kids can feel normal.

We didn't experience discrimination in the US, even during Covid. On the other hand, I am a little worried about going with my kids to China. My father told me that people in China believe the virus was made by the US and then spread in China. I fear that people may hate me when I go back.

Marc: Our marriage of ten years is actually like twenty years because we have been living twenty-four hours together. First, we ran our business together. Then in the US, we are at home together because of Covid and remote working.

Sofia: We go to the supermarket together. We pick up the baby together. Even when we eat buffet, I must accompany him if he needs to pick up some food. It's like our bodies are joined together.

Marc: Many of my friends, not only in interracial marriages, even those who married Indians, have cultural issues. Like you cannot eat this, you cannot wear that. And we never had any such problems.

Sofia: We don't have this problem. But if any young girl asks if marrying a foreigner is good, I will say, 'No!' Marrying a foreigner is much more difficult. It can only work out if you have a high EQ (Emotional Quotient). The difficulty comes from not sharing a common understanding. We argue for one or two hours, even over very small things. All things being equal, same quality, same personality, then I'll choose the Chinese, not Indian. There is too much scope for misunderstanding otherwise.

Once, before visiting a relative in Wuhan, we shopped for fruits to gift them. My father went with us. As he paid, I signalled Marc to go and pay instead. He said, 'Why? Your father is already paying?' But we Chinese know the reason, it is our culture.

Another time, we drove to the countryside to see my bedridden uncle. In the car, my father and I discussed how his son and daughter-in-law mistreated him. Then Marc suddenly said, 'Stop the car. I will never go to their house.' I asked why. He said, 'Because they are bad people. Why should I visit them?' In the end, he never went inside their house. We had to tell many lies to cover it up.

Marc: All these are small things.

Sofia: Life is made of all small things. He is very good at significant matters. But in small things, he is full of flaws.

I think Indian men are more macho than Chinese men. For example, he is not emotionally expressive. After a fight, he does not pacify me. When I am sick, he does not show care the way I have seen many Chinese men do. Seeing my father, I took this for granted and forgot to look for this in my future partner. My mother-in-law has similar complaints about my father-in-law. Perhaps Marc's behaviour comes from his father. So, I kind of forgive him. But then, he is not macho in other ways. He does all the housework. He consults me before making big decisions. He takes care of my family, his family, and our kids. He is a good man. I am learning to care less about small things.

But still, we argue a lot over our kids' education. If he were Chinese, we would have reached an agreement easily on such matters. For him, everything is fine. If I let him handle the kids for ten minutes, you can be sure the TV will be on. And if the kids want to go to bed late, 10 p.m., 11 p.m., or whatever time is always acceptable for him. And in the morning, if they cough just once, he would say, 'No need to go school today.'

Marc: The school will send them back anyway if they cough there.

I train the kids for their manners instead, like not throwing dirty socks and shoes around. I want them to have good manners.

Sofia: But if Marc hears some parents saying that their kids can write full sentences, he will come back and say to the kids, 'Why can't you do what other kids do?'

In China, our generation knows that 'Every kid is different. Every kid is special. No need to compare with others. Don't give them pressure.' But he still thinks like my parent's generation. That's why it would be easier if both of us were Chinese.

Marc: But all things being equal, I will still choose Chinese. The Indian girls never cared to talk to me anyway.

Our marriage is made in heaven. My biggest achievement in life is to have Sofia. Last year, my parents caught Covid and were unconscious. My relatives told me, 'Listen, Covid is spreading everywhere. If you come to India now, you may also catch it. Your parents are already old. They have already lived their life. You have kids to take care of. Don't come here.' I wanted to go, but I felt vulnerable. Then Sofia told me, 'Go. Go right now. When the kids grow up, what will they think? My father left my grandparents to die. What example are you setting for them?' She gave me this strength when I was chained to my emotions. I suddenly had all the courage and did all I could do. Hospitals were tight at that time. But I managed to get my father in the ICU for a month. My parents survived.

A friend of mine faced the same situation. But he didn't go back. In the end, his mother died of Covid. He called me and cried. I realized that I had the same weakness as him. Only because of Sofia could I save my parents. If she didn't give me the strength, I would have regretted it all my life.

Sofia: This is again because I feel very safe in my heart. Whatever happens, let's face it together. Marriage is the joining of two families. We are now one and the same family. His parents are old, so I urged them to sell their house in India and come and live with us in the US. We have always been very good together. But I'm worried we can't take care of them well. In Chinese, a saying goes, 'Even the most dutiful children fail you if you are bedridden for too long.' Healthcare in the US is very expensive and ineffective, especially in emergency situations. So, for now, my parents-in-law will live next to my father in China. It will be easier to manage as we have connections there, and my father can check on them daily. They have lived in China before and really love the place. We'll see how things go.

As for ourselves, Marc and I want to return to China when the kids reach eighteen and don't need us any more. We want to die in China. Not US, not UK, but China. That is where our hearts belong.

VI

Not all interracial relationships work out. Studies in the US show that divorce rates are higher for interracial couples. No such studies, however, have been done for Indian–Chinese relationships, both of whose cultures have a bias against separation. But when such relationships do not work out, how tempting is it to form new stereotypes—to blame the separation on another's ethnicity? Or how surprised are we by ourselves, to have fallen for someone who does not fit the ideal image?

It's Not About Race, but Personality

Story of Melany (name changed), twenties, Singaporean–Chinese. She lives in Singapore.

Melany: I was attracted to Indian men. But after having two Indian boyfriends, I learned my lesson and deliberately avoided dating Indians. Now, I have an Italian boyfriend.

I grew up in Singapore. I was rather meek in my early years. I was bullied and made fun of in school. But sometimes, I could also rebel against traditions. My parents would then nag me, 'Why are you not this? Why are you not that?' Growing up, I feared living the typical life of every other Singaporean— marrying their childhood sweetheart and settling down to buy a BTO[17].

I always found Chinese boys a turn-off. They were shy, reserved, and boring. As for the occasional opinionated ones, I found them more arrogant than charismatic. Chinese boys didn't seem to find me attractive as well.

Indian men, on the other hand, know how to work their characters. They seem flamboyant, with a lot of positive vibes. And yet, they were not so crazy over the top as the Caucasians. Indian culture has always intrigued me. It is very different from all that I was familiar with, but also had similarities with my

---

[17] Built-To-Order public housing in Singapore, the young generally need to be married to become eligible.

Chinese culture that emphasized tight-knitted families. So, being an Asian girl, I found Indians more attractive, comforting, and relatable. I was most attracted to their confidence and opinionated nature. Maybe deep down, I wanted to be like them.

I met my first Indian boyfriend online. He was confident and dominating. I was very attracted to him for that. We had instant chemistry. He was completely bald and had no facial hair. These gave him a clean look. He was very muscular, so he looked protective.

He had grown up in India but had spent his formative years in the US He came to Singapore in his thirties for work. He was very independent and only occasionally visited his parents. His parents were Hindus, but he was an atheist. Few of his friends were Indian. Most were Westerners. I used to joke that he's like a coconut: brown (Indian) outside, white (Western) inside. Perhaps because of this duality, he often wrestled with himself. The Indian and the American took turns to appear in him. One moment, he would want to take control, and like a stereotypical Indian man, he would want me to be submissive. The next moment, he would be like a Caucasian, demanding for me to be independent, not 'needy'. He didn't like Indian girls for being very 'dramatic' and 'difficult to handle', and he didn't like Western women for being 'loud'. So all his ex-girlfriends were east Asians. According to him, Chinese women were genuine, domesticated, and easier to 'manage'. Perhaps, I fit into his perception of Chinese girls. I often heard that men who are not confident look for a weaker party to 'manage'. If the girl is educated and opinionated, she will be challenging and demanding. Men find such girls scary. Perhaps, he was not as confident as I thought.

I wish I could meet both his requirements. But I, too, struggled a lot with my duality. Part of me wanted to follow traditions, as my parents expected. The other part of me wanted something different—like dating someone from a different culture. There is excitement in an interracial relationship. This boyfriend was my doorway to a new world. With him, I got to explore life in new ways I otherwise had no gut for, break away from my usual circles, and interact with people I otherwise wouldn't. We travelled to nearby countries, drank during the day, and did things uncommon for Singaporeans. Most of my friends wouldn't understand why any couple would spend two hours just reading a book in a café, just like we did at times.

But while this experience was unique, it was also intimidating. Often, I was the only Chinese girl in his gatherings. I would get overwhelmed. At such parties, everyone knew each other and talked within their circle. Everyone seemed older than me and well-established. They were open-minded and nice to me but were uninterested in getting to know me. Perhaps they didn't need new friends. As such, I didn't feel particularly welcomed. And I had nothing much to talk about with anyone. My boyfriend wasn't good at helping me in such situations. He would say, 'I want to catch up with my friends. You just mingle. You'll be fine yourself anyway.' But it was difficult. I was very young. I tried my best to fit in, only to realize that there was little I could do. Perhaps, that was only because I came from a different background.

But I did not experience any resistance from his family. They were very happy—'At least he's not gay!' They had been worried for him because he had not been in any serious relationship for a long time. And I was the first girl he took back to India.

My friends, on the other hand, liked him. He was sociable and knew how to read the room. My parents were against our relationship, especially because of the difference in religion. They were also uncomfortable with his race. They asked, 'Why can't you get a normal Chinese boy?'

He was also noncommittal, from the very start. He dictated our meeting frequency to be only once every week. He wanted space. I was always patient and understanding even though I wanted to meet him much more often, 'Okay, I know you need time for your work. If you want to meet, I am always here for you.' My mum often asked, 'He doesn't want to settle down. It has been four years. What's his plan?' He had earlier told me that he had never imagined himself in a relationship. But the naïve and adventurous me thought I could be 'the one' for him—the saviour who could change him and make him settle.

Over time, his dominance—something I was attracted to earlier—was why our relationship didn't work out. I felt very stifled. I avoided conflicts. In times of disagreement, I would be the one who always gave in. I would be the first to apologize even when it was not my fault. Being eight years older than me, he knew how to twist situations to his benefit. His way became the only way to approach a problem. My mum could tell that I was deeply unhappy. Slowly, we drifted apart.

I sought a psychiatrist's help after our breakup. Then, I better understood the dynamics of our relationship. He was a stubborn person stuck in his way of thinking. He would get angry for small things, like if the food in a restaurant didn't match its picture. But I am an empathetic person, and my strength is in giving. I gave my time and emotions, and he fed off my energy. When he felt anxious or stressed, I was his stabilizer, helping him to see new perspectives. This always made our dates stressful. I would never know if it would be a good or bad day. When things happened, I had to calm him down. But if I calmed him down the wrong way, he would lash out at me, 'You don't even understand.' But what could I say? Anything I did or did not do would be wrong.

My second boyfriend was an Indian too, but a Malaysian–Indian. He looked the complete opposite of the earlier one.

He was short. He had a lot of facial hair. Coming out of a noncommittal relationship, his sense of being a family man felt comforting. I wanted to settle down, and he seemed to be the type that settles down. But he also had those same traits, charisma, and dominance. And I fell for them again. He was so self-assured that my friends thought that he was actually a big show-off. But I knew he was not, he just had a certain way of asserting his points.

I attributed his mannerisms to the culture he came from. He was from the Sindhi community. Their community is very tight and small, formed mostly of business-minded people. So, they have a culture of comparing with each other. His friends—mostly Malaysian–Indians, Indian Indians, and American–Indians—were also like him. They were loud and talkative. At their gatherings, I felt overwhelmed by their high energy. I could hardly get in a word. They had little interest in knowing me—these gatherings were their time to catch up with each other. I became quieter and quieter. Then I started to withdraw from these parties.

Compared to my earlier boyfriend, he was much more 'Indian', much more traditional. Family and friends were critical to him. If we were to get married, he wanted me to be more involved in his social circles and family structures. This was scary. But I was also excited. I wanted to adapt and try this new culture, rather than be stuck with a boring structured life.

However, unlike my first boyfriend, who was an atheist, this boy was a Hindu. My parents and I are Christians. Religion is important to us. When I told my parents about my first boyfriend, my dad's first question was about his religion. Deep down, I, too, would want my children to grow up as Christians. Also, can I live like a Hindu? Life without beef is unthinkable. I liked to challenge my boundaries, but would it be too much? I was constantly on the fence between change and tradition.

Learning from my earlier experience, I decided not to rush too far into this relationship. I wanted to take it slow, to get to know each other and learn whether he was the right one. But, he complained that our relationship wasn't moving fast enough. He wanted to get married quickly, but perhaps he didn't see that happening fast enough with me. He went back to Malaysia once Covid restrictions were lifted. He stayed there for a long time, contacting me very rarely. I ended the relationship and cut my loss early. I had allowed my first relationship to go on for four years, even when we argued every week. This time, I chose not to repeat this mistake. I stopped it just after one year. Soon, he married a girl he had not known for long.

We spoke once after our breakup. He said, 'Don't make this experience mar our Indian men. Most Indian men are good.' I said maybe I would try something new. He said, 'So you are going to cancel off one of the largest sample sizes of men, and date white Caucasian men?' I was so offended.

I do have a bias against Indians now. I know my bias stems from a sample size of two. I do not like stereotypes because race itself cannot define relationships. But I saw recurring themes, and so I am cautious about Indians. I avoid mixing with them now. Still, I wish that I could be unbiased and fairer.

By then, I started to see the challenges in an interracial relationship. Society reacts to such relationships. In public transport, people—usually the older Chinese—used to stare at us and whisper. I knew they were judging us. I hate being judged. It makes me self-conscious. The unspoken was, 'Why can't this Chinese girl find anyone else?' or 'She does not value herself and just gives herself out to anybody.' I was very annoyed. Comfort in the same culture could indeed make relationships easier. I also began seeing good attributes in Chinese men and thought I might try them too. The best scenario would be to meet a Chinese guy who is very out there. But I didn't know anyone that type.

And yet, I still like to break out of my comfort zone. I need that newness. So, I ended up with an Italian, my current boyfriend. He is agnostic even though he was born a Catholic. My boyfriend and I had a conversation about religion and children. I found it a big deal that we could have an open conversation, respectfully and without being defensive. My friends can see that our relationship is working out. They like him as a person. I am no longer angry or upset. I no longer cry. I can be myself. I speak up when I need to. I don't feel the need to protect or defend myself. We can resolve things. Things fit well without even trying. Deep down, I know it's right. It's working. There is a lot of security and maturity in this relationship. We trust each other enough, and I know my feelings are safe. It was never the case in my previous relationships.

After all, I think it's not about race, but personality.

All Risks Didn't Matter Because I Really Liked Him

Story of Mehmet (name changed), forties, Indian. He lives in the United States.

Mehmet: Growing up in India—a society oblivious to all but heterosexuality—I never thought about my sexual orientation. I had crushes and sexual urges for other men. I couldn't express them openly. But I didn't understand what was happening. I suppressed all emotions. I focused only on education and career to over-compensate for my feelings. It was difficult.

I came to Singapore for undergraduate studies. We were a mixed lot—Indians, Indonesians, Chinese. It was a culture shock. I had never met any Chinese before. Everything was unfamiliar. I was homesick. For two months, I cried every day. I had no choice but to learn to move on.

I wasted most of my teens and twenties on one-sided relationships. I often fell for close friends, straight guys already in a relationship. There was this guy I fell madly in love with. I had butterflies in my tummy—my god, this is my perfect person. He had a girlfriend already. She was my friend as well. So sometimes, I promised myself I would not see this person any more. But I was addicted to him. I couldn't leave him. I felt so destroyed. I felt so abused. It took me six years to recover.

I had to see a therapist. I understood that I had developed a defence mechanism by going for such unachievable targets. I went after them knowing they would never reciprocate my love. This worked for me because I didn't want to admit openly that I was gay. But I kept creating hopeless situations for myself. I became the ultimate loser. I was wasting too much time. I didn't have to go through all that self-destruction and emotional rollercoasters. I could have instead focused on people I had a future with, people who would reciprocate my love both physically and emotionally. I could have found someone to marry, someone I could be comfortable facing the world with. I would have accepted myself faster and said this is who I am.

Besides these 'mental relationships,' I explored apps like Tinder and Grindr. The people there are just looking for sex, nothing more. I was too. This is how I split my life emotionally and physically. Grindr is a very disturbing place overall. Many people there were educated, well-accomplished professionals. But they have no manners. They behave just like animals, treating each other as nothing more than a piece of meat. It's a meat market. Everyone has the mindset, 'let's shop'. I did have a few memorable encounters through these apps, though. There was this Mexican who had become a good friend. We even explored a serious relationship, but it didn't work out due to the long distance. But such encounters are rare.

We meet all races in such an artificial setting of these apps. But there, race doesn't matter much. After all, we gays have a much smaller population to date with. So, we cannot be so choosy about race. 'Types' matter more to us—bears, chubby, hairy, six-packs, masculine, smooth skin, and effeminate. In addition, there is this component of being top, bottom, or versatile. Then there are the bisexuals. All these labels are physical. Only sexual and physical perceptions matter in such a transactional platform. With such a high degree of specialization, your pool becomes even smaller. People in the US have experimented a lot and taken their specializations to another level altogether. But I have only started to explore. Often, I don't understand what the hell is going on. I feel like a kid who has just started learning the alphabet while others are writing their PhD thesis. It is scary.

But race does matter in this world too. In Singapore, white men are the most popular, just like in the hetero-world. Because whites are thought to be successful, physically attractive, and tall. So most Asians—Chinese or Indian—are after them. The whites have a lot of choices here. They can go after anybody. And often, they go after the Chinese. Because when they come here, the whites want to explore something different. It's just like in the straight world of Singapore, white men going after Chinese girls.

So the white guys are after the Chinese, and the Chinese are after the white. For an Indian, this becomes tricky. We face racism. The whites and the Chinese body shame us, for being dark and for other reasons. There is also a perception of Indians being more closeted, the type who haven't experimented much. That means Indians are boring. The other races think, 'What the hell am I going to do with you?'

And then, Indians stand for low hygiene. After meeting Indians and Chinese, I realized the stereotype was true. Hygiene is very important to me, but many Indians never think that body odour is an issue; they don't apply any perfume. And they don't shave. They are hairy and sweaty. Their sweat glands behave differently—I don't know.

For me, I have a neutral look. So in Singapore, I could pass as a white or Middle-Eastern, or Malay. But when they ask my race, and I say Indian, I often get, 'I'm not interested,' or 'I'm only into Chinese men.' The same person was interested a moment ago when he saw my photo. What is the difference now? I am still the same person, no?

Some didn't believe me when I said I was an Indian. They then suspect me of being a scammer, someone with a fake account, using someone else's photo. It is a zero-trust transactional community. And people don't want to take any risks. They would then ask for multiple photos and photos of my body parts, 'Show me this, show me that.' It is like sitting in an interview.

But sometimes, it's about how exotic you are in a place. I could be totally unwanted in a country where nobody would reply to my messages but then be considered so exotic in another country that thousands would message me. Like in Taiwan, I was an exotic choice. Because there were so few Indians.

As for the Chinese gays in Singapore, they fall into multiple categories. One is the uneducated, low-income type. They are sex predators, and they don't like Indians at all. The other category is that of educated people who seem to be after something more substantial. The third belongs to the creepy old uncles in their sixties, typically bisexual or closeted gays, just looking for random fun. Chinese gay men are considered effeminate, because of their smooth skin. There's also a perception that Chinese men have smaller penises. Unfortunately, in the gay community, physical appearances mean a lot.

I once dated a Singaporean–Chinese. I was attracted to him. We hung out a few times and went out for dinners. But after we argued once, he completely blocked me out of his life. I don't know what happened. Maybe he was going through something I didn't know. After all, the gay community is emotionally volatile and very bipolar. People have extreme bursts of reactions. I have gone through that journey myself.

The other Chinese man I dated was when I was living in Taiwan. It was a random match through an app. He absolutely didn't fit my desired profile for an ideal partner. I always had this mindset of an arranged marriage to find someone you are most common with. Then the other person can blend well into your value system and family. Love will then ultimately happen. This approach is very scientific because the more risk factors in a relationship, the more un-commonalities, and the more the chances of a conflict. Love stays only when there is no conflict. It's exactly like in straight relationships.

With the Taiwanese guy, our first risk factor was food. I am a vegetarian and a foodie. I can't imagine any meat being eaten in my house. If the person I date is not a vegetarian, he should be open to becoming one. This pretty much ruled out all Chinese. Religion is another risk factor. The person has to be god-fearing, but not overly ritualistic like must go to mosque or church. Most Chinese are atheists or Christians. Some are Buddhists, but their Buddhism is very different from what we have in India. Cultural value is also a risk factor. I am from a collective society where it's important that we take care of the family and the elderly. I can't be with an individualistic person who only thinks about himself and puts his parents in old-age homes.

In an ideal world, I want to be married to someone. I have not told my parents about my sexual orientation, but I would love our families to embrace each other. On this note, white people will be off my list because they don't care about family as much. I want someone ambitious, well-educated, and driven, almost alpha, someone I identify with. I don't want to be a sugar daddy or marry a trophy husband who is just a showpiece. Finally, my partner should love children. I want to have kids, so it will be a problem if he doesn't want to. With all these considerations, only Indians seem to fit the bill.

But I bonded so well with this Taiwanese guy. He didn't tick most items on my checklist. He was not vegetarian. He wasn't alpha. He was very reserved, calm, quiet, and introverted. But we enjoyed our time together. We clicked. We felt physically attracted to each other. Despite our differences, we had many common values. Perhaps this was because we were in a similar state of life. We were both feeling emotionally vulnerable. We were both feeling stuck in Taiwan.

Eventually, he blocked me. I can understand why. He was twenty-five, I was forty-two. He had big ambitions. He wanted to focus on his career. But he also had to take care of his family. They were not rich, and he was their caretaker. This situation troubled him a lot. He felt vulnerable. Our relationship distracted him; it affected his mental health.

And then, I was about to leave Taiwan. I really hated Taiwan. I found everything about the place annoying. They were racist toward everybody, including other Chinese. The Taiwanese only love the Japanese. Even my Singaporean–Chinese friends felt marginalized in Taiwan. But despite all this, Taiwan embraces LGBT people. This open-mindedness was shocking, given how narrow-minded they were in other aspects. My partner hated Taiwan too. But he couldn't leave at that time. And the long distance was not his thing.

When we parted ways, I told him, 'My door is always open for you.' I find our story so amazing. We had so many differences. He was so far from my idea of an ideal partner. And then, all these risk factors didn't matter because I really liked him. That was all that mattered.

So we can have all our laundry lists for an ideal partner, but regarding matters of heart, we are still human beings.

We never know.

VII

And here is . . . our own story.

Thank You For Letting Me Become Me

Story of Yolanda Yu, forties, Chinese–Singaporean born in China, and Shivaji Das, forties, Indian–Singaporean born in India. They are married and live in Singapore.

Shivaji: I was born in Lumding—a small town of around 50,000 people—in the north-eastern state of Assam. We were Bengali-Hindus. Like my parents, most people in Lumding were Hindu migrants from Bangladesh. My father came from Dhaka, and my mother from Mymensingh. We were not rich, but in that town, we weren't considered poor either. We didn't have television till I was ten. Religious festivals—plenty around the year—stood for entertainment.

Home was that frog's small pond. We had little idea about the world outside. We ate only home-cooked food, only dishes from Dhaka cuisine. Arranged marriages were the norm, between people from the same caste, preferably between those who migrated from the same district in Bangladesh. Love marriage was considered the original sin. My parents gorged out endless instances of doom when someone married someone of their own choice. Their favourite villain was Michael Madhusudan Datta—the modernizing writer who was also the first Bengali to marry a European. 'See how he fell so sick and became so poor, karma for loving foreign culture so much. Bengali mother's English son. Never be like that.' If I listened to

English songs or said anything against our religious practices, out came Michael Madhusudan Dutta.

My parents doused me heavily in religion. Every day we recited prayers. Every evening they sang devotional songs and made me sit through them. They dressed me up like Krishna. They even believed I was the reincarnation of Shiva. All these made me a religious fanatic, as much as I could be as a toddler. But one day, the idol fell off its pedestal, literally. I was four years old then. I used to make crude clay idols of gods and goddesses to pray, and one day, the hand of the goddess Durga idol I had made broke. I couldn't fix it back, no matter how hard I tried. I went into a rage. Why couldn't a god fix itself? I threw away all the idols and framed prints of gods we had at home. I smashed the potteries used for religious offerings. I tore off all decorations from the prayer room. That was the beginning of my atheism and a certain aversion to my own culture.

After that, I listened to only English music. I read only English books. I watched only English films. At university, I was known as 'pseud,' a wannabe Western-minded sophisticate. But because of my academic and professional achievements, my parents didn't mind my insults to their gods, the loud metal music blasting off the speakers, my eating beef, or even my downplaying of my mother's cooking. By the time I reached high school, I had stopped hearing about Michael Madhusudan Dutta.

Yolanda: I was born in Shenyang, north-eastern China. Shortly after I was born, my father's job took us to live in a village. Most villagers there belonged to two or three local clans. My family was a complete outsider. I struggled to make friends.

My mother was a primary school teacher. Besides her day job, she cared for my paralysed grandpa, our farmland, my baby brother, and me. My dad, who often travelled for work, provided little help. Lugging me into her classroom was a convenient childcare option. But she was also a firm believer in 'starting early' as the key to future success. As a result, I started schooling at three while my classmates were already seven. My peers entered puberty while I stayed a 'baby'. Though I tried to gate crash their secretive discussions about womanhood, I was always an outsider.

Shivaji: I was an extroverted child, but as I grew up, I enclosed myself in my world. We rarely travelled. And I hated guests. But in my closed world, there were a lot of magazines, Soviet books that flooded non-aligned India in the eighties, and textbooks from my Catholic school, full of Western myths and legends. Also, there was our family's stamp collection, sourced from an uncle who worked at the postal services. In these stamps, I loved country names like Upper Volta or Magyar. These stories and stamps were my windows to the outside world. I yearned for an escape from my small town.

Yolanda: I, too, had a vast space in my small bubble. I was a hungry reader. I could recite Chinese poems before I could count. *Arabian Nights*, *Red Mansion*, Shakespeare, and the *Hunchback of Notre Dame*: I lived in a world of classics created by people who were long dead. While my parents often quarrelled because of our family business and my dad's affairs, my readings helped me escape all that emotional turbulence at home. I, too, fantasized about leaving my small town and going into the outside world.

Shivaji: And yet, I had only a vague idea about China, although we lived a mere 150 kilometres from the Tibetan border. My parents often talked about China, but only of their struggles during the 1962 war when Chinese forces nearly reached

Lumding, of how they ran to the bomb shelters the moment they heard the sirens, of how food became scarce and they were forced to live on potatoes. Even then, they expressed little animosity towards China. My parents would talk about Mao and Zhou Enlai as great leaders, of the Chinese people being poor just like us, and how the flooding of the Yellow River brought misery upon them year after year. The war was something that had happened long back, and a repeat was unimaginable. But my strongest memory of China is that of actors enacting Chinese soldiers in a television show about Indian military heroes. At school, we all delighted in imitating how they spoke in their heavily accented Hindi, 'Indians and Chinese are brothers. This is our land. Leave this land.'

At school, I had many friends among people we considered 'Chinki' or semi-Chinese. They were the so-called tribal people—the Nagas, Mizos, Bodos, Nepalis. We 'Aryans' said that, like the Chinese, these tribals ate snakes, spoke 'ching-chong-ching-chong,' had flat nose, flat face, and slitty eyes. When we reached puberty and became hirsute, we teased these smooth-skinned classmates. But I found their girls attractive. I loved those very eyes, facial bone structure, and skin.

Yolanda: India had a special place in my heart. My mom and I thought of India as exotic. Until today, my mom fondly remembers the sexy gypsy girl in the Indian movie *Caravan*. And I watched the TV drama *Journey to the West*[18] countless times. In one of the episodes, a devil-turned-Indian princess mesmerized me with her beautiful costume. Tagore's poems were another source of my fantasy of an exotic India. From these poems, I formed a magical image of India where women

---

[18] A fictional account of a pilgrimage trip to India by Tang Xuanzang, a Tang dynasty monk. The original book was a Chinese literature classic.

in braided hair covered with a delicate veil walked to the river accompanied by the melody of their anklet bells.

Shivaji: As I began working, I had more time for myself. I started reading a lot again. I got familiar with the works of Marx, Sartre, and Bakunin. I tilted heavily to the left. My mind raced through concepts like the oppression of family, base-superstructure, radical education and, of course, religion as the opium of the masses. I became even more curious about the world.

After working for two years in the US, I moved to Singapore. I began travelling extensively—Myanmar, Laos, Cambodia, and Indonesia. From someone who hated travelling, I became a person who looked at every opportunity to head out. As I began travelling, I realized I could feel attracted to people from any race.

And yet, I placed full faith in the concept of arranged marriage. I am short in stature, and because I went through the best universities in India, I was convinced that this traditional system, and not my own charm, would help me find a good match. So, once I reached the ripe age of twenty-eight, my parents gleefully put up matrimonial adverts for me in India. I shortlisted two possible matches and went all the way to India to meet them. Both got ticked off, rather quickly, by my pompous declarations of atheism, worried about what it could mean for our children in waiting. I vowed to never again look at this arranged marriage option. Seeing such strong reactions from both, I somehow felt certain that I wouldn't be able to live an entire life with an Indian Hindu. Back came with gusto, my childhood revulsion against my own culture.

I took things into my own hands and tried to find my own match. The filter I used to search was 'no religion' or 'atheist.' I met a few girls in Singapore, mostly Singaporean–Chinese.

And then I came across Yolanda, the first person from China I would date.

Yolanda: When I was fifteen, I received a scholarship to study in Singapore. My mother reacted with joy and fear. As a mother of a teenage girl, she had every reason to be cautious of the outside world. But there was another layer to this fear. We, north-eastern Chinese, call ourselves 'Guanwai'—people outside the Great Wall. We Guanwai are simple and trusting. Anyone inside the Great Wall was a 'Guanli', manipulative and cold-blooded, penny-wise, ever ready to short-change us Guanwais.

The university in Singapore offered some level of diversity. There were Singaporeans, Malaysian–Chinese, Malays, and Indians in my proximity. But English was a challenge for me. On orientation day, I couldn't understand the seniors' commands. They scolded me, and I broke down. The organizers feared retribution and exempted me from the rest of the orientation. I exempted myself from social life altogether. Later, when I couldn't follow the lectures, I opted out of all the classes. So even in the open world of Singapore, I weaved myself into a cocoon.

I became aware of this cocoon only after I started working. I developed a strong urge to understand the real world. This desire drove me to move into customer-facing jobs. I tried to acquire people skills. I built a circle of friends. I worked with people from all over the world and learned to appreciate individual differences.

By the time I met Shivaji, I had a thriving career as a recruiter. By then, I was open to people from any background, with any belief system. Coming out of a damaging relationship, I was all for a reset. I wanted someone trustworthy, intellectually engaging, and with an active lifestyle. And these things had nothing to do with people's backgrounds. I signed up for an online dating platform. There, I set up a height filter. My mom, like others in my hometown, gave a lot of importance to men's height. For once, I felt like fulfilling my mother's wishes.

On the platform, I met a British Catholic, a Malay Muslim, a Singaporean Buddhist, and a Hindu from India. The tallest man was a Malaysian–Chinese, over six feet. I was so bored of him that I could hardly bear to finish the second drink. Why waste time on boring people? Why waste my paid membership to meet boring people? I removed the height filter. Had I not, Shivaji and I would have never met.

Shivaji: I, too, didn't see her on that platform for a few months that I had been on it already. I had set a minimum age as a filter. Her profile showed up only after she turned twenty-eight.

Yolanda: One day, a message there caught my attention. His height was the same as mine, meaning he was not 'tall enough.' He said he was a writer-wannabe. I encountered the word 'wannabe' for the first time. Either you are something, or you are not. But here's a 'wannabe!' I liked the humour.

I suggested to him that we get on the phone. He was travelling soon and asked to meet after he came back. I pushed him to meet before the trip. Looking back, I am always surprised by my boldness that day. I behaved the way I did because I had zero expectations of him being a prospect. So, all my subconscious ideas of traditional gender dynamics didn't manifest itself.

Shivaji: By then, I had a more informed idea of China. In my mind, it was a fabled land. It was the land of Mao. It was the land of fellow atheists. I thought of Chinese culture as one of the most idiosyncratic—in food habits, clothing, or music.

Such was my state of mind—an interest in the developing world, an urge to explore the unfamiliar—that it was perfect timing. So, I was very excited about meeting Yolanda.

Yolanda: For me, he had nothing to do with India. At work, I met all sorts of Indians: British–Indians, southern Indians, northern Indians, and north-eastern Indians. They were intelligent people. Some were modern and open. Some were religious and old-fashioned. Some were trustworthy. Some were slippery. Some were handsome. Some were unflattering. One of my university friends married an Indian. And I recall asking her about her 'different' husband. She had said, 'He is just an ordinary person, same as us, really.'

To me, an Indian origin said nothing about the person. I was also unimpressed when Shivaji mentioned his background in consulting, IIT[19], and IIM[20]. The ignorant me didn't know these social signals for a high IQ (Intellectual Quotient).

He nonetheless left a strong impression on me. He was very well-read, a 'walking encyclopedia'. And he had strong, almost eccentric opinions. He was an atheist and anarchist. He didn't believe in the concept of family and dreamed of building a school system with complete equality. I couldn't fully process these, but they were a refreshing blow to my mind. Until then, I had never given religion or social structure careful thought.

His unusual travel experiences also fascinated me. From our first meeting to every day after, it always felt like I was following him on a treasure hunt with my starry eyes and an open heart.

Shivaji: We talked for hours—about the oppression of family, base and superstructure, radical education and, of course,

---

[19] Indian Institute of Technology: Best university in India.

[20] Indian Institute of Management: Best business school in India.

religion as the opium of the masses. Soon I realized that despite her being from the land of Mao, Yolanda knew little about all these. But she was refreshingly open-minded. She listened eagerly, challenged the concepts, and at times agreed wholeheartedly. She introduced me to the Chinese literary classics and opened my eyes to a fascinating culture.

Yolanda: He *liked Journey to the West* but despised the *Red Mansion* as over-depicting a frail melancholic woman who kept coughing pretentiously. I was hurt. This girl from *Red Mansion* was my childhood favourite.

Shivaji: We travelled through wretched places and were delighted to spend nights in hotels with stained beds, creaking doors, and ghostly characters. We watched movies together— *The Adventures of Iron Pussy* by Apichatpong Weerasethakul and *Stalker* by Tarkovsky. We could appreciate both the slapstick and the artful. She made me watch anti-Japanese films from China, and we both laughed a lot at how the Japanese villain was always portrayed as hyperventilating bald spectacled men. With her, I enjoyed every experience more than I did alone. With her, I felt my life would not be one of mind-numbing compromises—something I had always felt very uncomfortable about. It was a big deal. Her maturity, self-assurance and openness were exhilarating. I had found a rare treasure. With her, I could breathe without restraint. This Chinese girl was not the Stalinist woman I had romanticized about, but this was the person I fell in love with.

Within a year of being together, we passed hints to each other about the prospect of getting married. Together, we went to India, so Yolanda could get a more thorough experience of living with my parents and other relations. First, we went to my sister's house in Assam. My sister's husband was especially happy to have Yolanda in the family. 'See how my kids are now forced to talk to a foreigner, he said. 'This will do much good to their confidence.'

While we were certain that people in Assam wouldn't find Yolanda any different from Nagas or Bodos, they still did. A group of youngsters were idling at a traffic junction, a common way to kill time in Assam. One of them screamed in Assamese when he saw Yolanda passing by, 'No eyes, no eyes.' My sister ran up to the group and gave them a verbal thrashing. They ran away, their tail behind their legs.

Yolanda: The silliness and happiness in his sister's house made me blend in easily. For the first time, I didn't feel like an outsider. After all, we shared a common language—laughter. And our walk to the Brahmaputra River in the dim evening light gave me a strange comfort—this was the same river which flows in China, its Chinese name is Yaluzangbu[21].

Shivaji: Next, we visited Mumbai, where my parents and my other sister were. I was unsure how my mother would react, though. All along, she had been saying that 'Marrying a foreigner is risky because they divorce at the slightest conflict.' But she stopped saying that once she became aware of our relationship. Perhaps this was because of her strong belief that saying something bad makes it happen for real. That's why in our house, no one used to utter names of diseases like 'cancer'.

Yolanda: In Mumbai, I wanted to try out my 'sofa test'. I had this fear that once married, my life would be too bonded, that I would always have to sit 'like a lady' on the house sofa, unable

---

[21] Translated from Yarlung Tsangpo in Tibetan.

to lie down on it if I wanted to. I found this thought unnerving, even though I rarely lay on the sofa.

In their Mumbai household, everything had its designated time and space. There was a natural flow of life: they woke up, showered, and performed puja[22]. In the afternoon, they took a nap, then sat around for tea and talked. His parents and sister's family could speak English. But when they sat together, they'd speak Bengali among themselves. Shivaji tried his best to be our interpreter, but he couldn't do it all. A lot of times, I was left not knowing what was happening. But I just eased into the rhythm. Every day flowed the same way. But it was never boring. In the spaciousness, we spread ourselves out and excavated the day's gems: smiles, recalling the past, humouring each other in the present. In this atmosphere, I lay on the sofa countless times. So did they, and passed the 'sofa test'.

Listening to Tagore and Nazrul songs was also part of their routine. These songs would play for hours. I, too, began to enjoy these soul-soothing songs. Tagore, my childhood favourite, dominates Bengali culture. I learned to sing his song 'Ami Chini Go Chini Tomare.' It means, 'You stranger from a distant land, you are familiar to me.' Chini meant familiarity, but also sugar, and Chinese. One day, we were listening to this song, and my mum-in-law put her soft hands on mine. 'You sweet foreigner girl.'

Shivaji: I proposed to Yolanda in our neighbourhood park while riding a manual ferris wheel. As two operators of the wheel jumped in sequence, grabbing the bar and pulling it down to keep it turning, I asked her, 'Yes or no?' She said, 'Yes, yes, yes,' looking scared and distracted by this unfamiliar contraption. Soon after that, we got whistled out of the park by the security

---

[22] Prayer and religious offerings in India.

guards, who were forever on the watch for any couple who were getting too close to each other. Once we returned home, my sister told us she had just tested negative for breast cancer. It was a happy night. We told them about what had happened in the park. My parents immediately assembled some desserts and organized a small ceremony to give us blessings. We were thus engaged.

Yolanda: I was delighted with that ceremony. It was probably the only one we ever had. I enjoyed getting dressed in saree with a bindi on my forehead. I enjoyed kneeling before a fierce and mysterious Kali goddess immersed in incense smoke. I enjoyed the attention I received when walking in the neighbourhood, feeling like a new wife, a foreign wife. It was like a carnival. But it was brief. I felt I got a lesser deal in the cultural aspect because Shivaji was against all rituals.

Shivaji: We headed for China too, to get her mom's approval. This was more complicated. The first issue was clothing. We went during winter, and seeing my packing, Yolanda said that people in China wouldn't be impressed by my slim-fits. They like people dressed as Michelin Man during winter—all padded up. Otherwise, it is seen as a case of penury. I obliged and bought oversized jackets, double mittens, and even innerwear—which I hated wearing.

Yolanda: Michelin Man was the right way to enter our harsh winter. Before the invention of lightweight winterwear, only the poor would show up shivering in slim-fit. Maybe there is a thing in my culture about masculinity. The Manchu[23] people were originally good at archery, wrestling, and horse riding.

---

[23] A minority race, mostly residing in north-eastern China.

These traits helped them to take over China and form the Qing Dynasty. But the modern north-eastern men are no longer good at that. They are good at giving bold speeches in restaurants reeking of alcohol and cigarette smell. What remains is that one needs to look 'bulky' to gain respect. My mom never complained about Shivaji being an Indian. What she did complain about was that he was not fat. 'If he doesn't have the height, then some weight would help to build gravitas.'

On this critical topic of height, Shivaji argued that smart people like Deng Xiaoping and Napoleon were not tall. Then he said, 'Short people are smarter because they hid half of themselves underground.' When I told my mum these, she laughed with endorsement. Deng Xiaoping was the key.

My dad passed away when I was nineteen. He was a very traditional man with strong views of clans and races. It would have been much harder to get his approval. But he was also a very curious and adventurous person. So who knows? Life offered me no chance to test.

Shivaji: That was my first trip to China. There was a certain bustle in the streets, even in that small town in north-east China. People were always curious yet helpful and welcoming. Sometimes, I was dragged away by strangers for selfies. Sometimes, passers-by just wanted to hold my hand. Shopkeepers called me 'Hai-zi' (child). People took me for an African, or Afghan, or Uighur. The food was great too. That was the time I ate everything. Everyone I met would prepare a lavish meal. I munched up all the trotters, intestines, and worms. I spoke little but smiled a lot. Everything went fine till the last day.

It was Yolanda's mother's birthday. To celebrate, we went to a family-style karaoke. Just after leaving home, I realized I had left my wallet behind. Yolanda said that it would be all right since her family would pay anyway. But everyone started looking at me when it was time to pay. Yolanda and her brother nudged me. It suddenly became clear that the cultural expectation was for the would-be son-in-law to pay and win the mother's heart.

Yolanda: There are a few discrepancies in our memories. I didn't tell him my family would pay. Absent-minded, I probably just didn't foresee what was to come. There is a certain expectation of the sons-in-law and would-be in my culture. Their willingness to pay indicates their willingness to be the man of this family. And I only learned in hindsight that our society was very codified. On each occasion and configuration, there is a way one 'is supposed to' behave. I was bad at recalling the social codes but panicked thinking of the punishment. As a chronic outsider to my culture, I was unfamiliar with any social codes, especially those for men. Having grown up learning all the social expectations, Chinese boys would know what to do. But Shivaji came from a different culture.

I also remember that my mother did not take offence, at least on this occasion. And I wonder how many of these social codes only existed in my mind.

Shivaji: Her mother certainly didn't expect me to pay. I was her foreign guest, after all. But Yolanda and her younger brother did. It was all a misunderstanding, but I was angry at Yolanda for not considering this when I told her about my wallet. When I asked her for an explanation, she started crying. My mother-in-law didn't like this part about her crying at my words. She took it as a sign that I could be abusive towards her daughter.

The next day, my mother-in-law wanted to have a candid conversation with me. We talked on our way to the airport, with Yolanda as the interpreter. Unfortunately, it was a very long car ride.

Yolanda: My mom's exact question was, 'Who will you choose to live with, my daughter or your parents, if they can't live together?' And Shivaji replied sternly that such a rhetorical question deserved no answer.

Shivaji: Yolanda, already stressed, translated all these exchanges verbatim with no filters.

Yolanda: I could empathize with both of them. My mom had a terrible experience with her mother-in-law. Hearing that I might have to live with my parents-in-law, she desperately wanted to prevent a similar disaster in my life. As for Shivaji, I knew it was a very hard and unfair question related to his parents. But I felt angry and hurt. Neither of them bothered to be nicer, for my sake. I sat between the two I love, facilitating their fight, crying. Their anger and mistrust found no border. Language ceased being a barrier.

Luckily, they reconciled, soon after we got married. Now my mom often says that I made a great decision to marry a man of character and kindness.

Shivaji: As for Yolanda and me, we resolved the misunderstanding within the six-hour flight back to Singapore. Two months later, we got married.

Yolanda: When I called my mom saying, 'I'm getting married,' her immediate answer was, 'To whom?' She had not expected us to continue dating each other after that fight. I had forgotten to update her.

Shivaji: We organized a secular wedding in Singapore, simplified to signing of papers followed by dinner with friends. We chose Indonesian cuisine to keep it neutral to our respective cultures. Yolanda wore a saree. I wore a Chinese shirt bought from Singapore's Chinatown street-market. I found it strange to buy a wedding shirt from a shop selling touristy junk, but that seemed to be the only option. The shirt was heavy and hot. It made me sweat a few litres that day. When we looked at the wedding pictures, we found that we were always laughing with abnormally wide grins, looking very different from our usual selves.

Yolanda: There was a sense of freedom. We had the costumes without the rituals, and culture without obligations.

The wedding was simple. We didn't rent any wedding cars. I flagged down a taxi and got to the wedding restaurant. Some of my guests were shocked. 'Oh, this taxi driver is lucky.'

But the day felt like a dream come true. In my university days, I was fascinated by an advertisement poster of an Indian bride. She was wearing ten kilos of jewellery. An enormous ring ran through her nose, dangerous and beautiful. Like her, I, too, married in a red saree, sans the ten-kilo jewellery.

Shivaji: Our wedding was when my parents and in-laws met for the first time. Restricted by cumbersome Chinese–English–Bengali translations, their exchanges were limited to saying nice things. Somehow, my father formed a close bond with Yolanda's brother. They kept shaking each other's hands. Even now, both ask about the well-being of the other every time they speak to us.

Yolanda and I have been to India many times since. I wanted to show her how diverse India is. We have been to the north-eastern states, parts of Rajasthan, Maharashtra, Gujarat, Kolkata, and the holy city of Varanasi. And despite my irritation at the communal tone of politics and casteism prevalent in India, there is a certain relaxed warmth, generosity, and cultural sophistication that has made me love travelling around the country. Both Yolanda and our daughter are welcomed wholeheartedly in India. Strangers ask for pictures posing next to us. Our child gets some extra love for her mixed origins.

I have also been to China many times since, and every time has been rather enjoyable. The landscape—deserts, high mountains, river valleys, shiny cities—is the most dramatic. I remain immensely interested in the quirks of Chinese culture too. I can quote some Li Bai and Du Fu. I can recognize over 1000 Chinese characters now. I even gave a speech in Mandarin during Yolanda's brother's wedding. The weirdest thing I have done was to wear a full-body spandex—in bright red with golden dragon prints—on the occasion of Chinese New Year. Wearing it, I felt like a clown fresh out of a circus.

Now I have a more evolved view of China. I see a traditional Chinese mindset as a carbon copy of Indian one—male privilege, mandatory reverence for elders, an idea of racial purity, and family over anything else. Even the modern Chinese mindset is not too different from an Indian's—populist-nationalist, strong inferiority complex, blames the 'West' for all ills, and reveres praise from the least credible 'Western' source. And while unlike Indians, most Chinese are not religious, they are no less superstitious than Indians—my mother-in-law deletes any accidental picture of tombs from her mobile phone, thinking it would bring misfortune.

But there is this 'Chinese' expectation of me as a son-in-law that I have found hard to rise up to. Among us Bengalis, a son-in-law is akin to God, with dedicated festivals for him like Jamai-Shashti. In China, it is the exact opposite. Their ideal son-in-law is akin to an observant service staff who is always on guard to rectify the slightest inconvenience for his in-laws. When the in-laws visit, he must stock up the fridge so much that the door can't be closed. He must gift branded items that send strong social signals. But why waste food? Why waste money on social signals? I wasn't expecting Jamai-Shashti, but I rebelled whenever I was supposed to cater to such a contrasting expectation.

I am perplexed by my behaviour. On one hand, I am very curious and interested in various cultures—rituals, social obligations, and role plays. I actively seek them out in my travels. And yet I feel so repulsed when it comes to practising them myself. My extreme rationality only allows me to be an observer; it rejects the role of a forced participant.

Yolanda: That applies to me, too. I find the Indian rituals fancy. But I would rebel if anyone forced me to spend an hour every day performing these same rituals. I know many Indian wives have to do it, willingly or not.

His parents live with us for a few months every year. They don't expect me to act as an Indian wife should. I can just be myself. They also never imposed anything on Shivaji. Such a clear boundary is extremely rare in Chinese society, where families are full of blurred boundaries. So I thoroughly enjoy being with them and taking care of them.

Shivaji: In our own life as a couple, culture has been less of a force. Both of us are not the best representative of our own culture. I have been living overseas for twenty years, Yolanda, twenty-five. And as time passes, Yolanda and I have been drifting further from our own cultures. Now, nothing about her strikes me as being particularly Chinese. Well, except for her periodic bouts of addiction to munching sunflower seeds. And although there is a lot of that Bengali in me—a certain pride in Bengali cultural achievements, a love for Bengali desserts— my turning atheist has taken away a big part of the Bengali cultural expression in our day-to-day life. At home, there are no religious idols, no prayers and no offerings, no celebration of festivals even, things that occupy so much of Hindu life. When my parents visit us, they follow our pattern.

And when we had our child, we gave her a name by running a computer simulation of randomly generated syllables. This was done deliberately to keep her name free from any cultural association.

Yolanda: There is still a lot of cultural backwater in our relationship. It's beyond rituals and social codes. Take our long debates over TCM[24]. I used to believe that Western medicine only addresses the symptoms and not the root cause. Shivaji would say any medicine, TCM or Western, must fulfil statistical control group tests. I complain about him eating too much salt. He would say that's in his genes, an adaptation to humid weather in the Bangladesh plains.

We don't eat much Chinese food at home, mainly because Chinese cuisine offers limited options for a vegetarian diet. We have Indian, Thai, Indonesian, Mexican, and Mediterranean foods on our dining table. I wholeheartedly love naan, most of the daals, and some of the home recipes from my mom-in-law. And I also fell for the sinful pleasures of rasmalai and other desserts. I never used to like sweets before we met. But Bengalis take a lot of pride in their desserts. I couldn't understand why such prestige—aren't their desserts just made of milk, sugar, and flour, boiled and stirred repeatedly? Nonetheless, my tongue took a liking for these.

I had even tried my hands at curry, literally. At the first meal after our wedding, I was still wearing my crystal bridal nails. Sadly, the turmeric in the curry stained its white flowers and was extremely hard to wash off. After that experience, I quit eating with my hands.

---

[24] Traditional Chinese Medicine.

I learned a few Bengali words and could make out what a conversation was about. But the complexity of their numbers killed my interest, and I am now limited to saying, 'How are you?' and 'I'm good, and you?' in Bengali.

If there was a 'culture war' at home, then it seems like I have lost, at least on the food front. But it was not Indian culture that won. It was science, evidence-based philosophy, and intellect that won. At the core, Shivaji had more Western values than traditional Indian values. And I have come to embrace these values. Now, I even try to steer my mom away from TCM when she needs to get a proper check-up.

Shivaji: I wouldn't say I have 'Western' values. I am 'largely rational.' There is no 'Western' trademark over rationality.

Yolanda: He influenced me the most, not with his opinions, but with his ways of forming opinions. I have become a lot more opinionated since. For example, becoming a vegetarian was thanks to his role modelling. But I did my own research, thought it through, and became vegetarian on my remit. And now I am honouring my own conviction, not his. To me, this was a big step in my personal growth. And it could only happen because he gave me a lot of space. He became a vegetarian eleven years ago. And in all those years I ate meat, he didn't comment even once about what I should do. He just did what he thought was right and left me to do what I thought was right.

Shivaji: My mother-in-law was shocked when I turned vegetarian, purely out of conscience. When Yolanda had pitched my case to her mother, she had said, 'He eats everything, no food restrictions.' And from someone who deliberately ate beef to challenge my birth-religion, I made this sudden 180-degree shift within a year of getting married, not even eating eggs, a staple of Chinese cooking. Even my Indian acquaintances say, 'How can a Bengali be a vegetarian?' So now, I can't taste the highlights of my mother's cooking any more: dimer kaliya (thickened egg curry), mutton curry, mustard prawn. I can't taste the highlights of my mother-in-law's cooking either: egg dumplings, fried silkworms. After Yolanda also became vegetarian, she too was denied the same.

My parents blame me for Yolanda's conversion, 'She sacrificed for you like Gandhari,' referring to the character from the *Mahabharata* who blindfolded herself for life after marrying a blind king. But it was Yolanda's own choice.

Yolanda: Shivaji also opened my eyes to the vast world of books outside China. With this, I lost interest in Chinese literature. Chinese writers are silenced under heavy censorship. There is nothing provocative or fundamentally reflective on a society or humanity level. Media is pretty much a walking dead. I extensively read in English now. Considering that I grew up immersed in the Chinese language, this change is huge.

But Chinese culture is making a big comeback in our house because of our daughter. I built her a Chinese library with poetry, paintings, and stories. She speaks fluent Chinese and started to read and write in Chinese much earlier than in English. She loves Chinese costumes, listens to our ancient poems, and declares herself 'a little girl from China.' Because of Covid, she hasn't been to China yet. She keeps asking me when. Hopefully, we will be going soon.

Marrying a foreigner created a distance between me and my culture. This distance is beneficial because I could see the world from a non-China-centric view. It also allowed me to reconnect with Chinese culture. While I may partially disengage, I now feel a new intimacy with it in my heart. I had been worried that because of my marriage to a foreigner and our life in Singapore, my daughter will lose the connection with my side of the family. So I immensely treasure my daughter and my mother chatting seamlessly with one another, as if there was never another culture separating them.

My fantasy for India has worn out as I understood more about the country. The image of the girl fetching water is no longer associated with beauty in my mind. It now raises concerns about how low caste and minorities can have safe access to water. I also join him in laughing and angering at the country's ridiculous events, just like I would about China. For me, it's no longer an 'other culture,' but mine, too.

Shivaji: Similarly, because of our daughter, the Bengali culture has found a bigger space at home. I speak to my child in Bengali. I have got her the Bengali classics I read as a child – *Abol Tabol* (absurd poems), *Nonte Fonte* comics, children's songs by Antara Chowdhuri. It is out of practical considerations and has little to do with catering to my pride in Bengali culture. The Bengali language seems grammatically closer to other Indo-European languages than English. Since Bengali has many loan words from Sanskrit, Arabic and Persian, I also found it easy to pick up other languages. So perhaps if she learns Bengali, she will find it easier to pick up many other languages.

As for outsiders, people in China or India have never reacted negatively to us for marrying outside. But people in Singapore and other countries have. In Singapore, a few Chinese taxi drivers have said, 'Oh, you are married to a Chinese. You are very lucky.' Occasionally, we get stared at by older Chinese people when we take public transport. I stopped going to our favourite vegetarian restaurant in Singapore once the owner told Yolanda, 'He is good. He is the fair skin type.' A shopkeeper in Indonesia—an old Chinese man—once told Yolanda, 'Why couldn't you find a Chinese man?' In South Korea, a middle-aged Chinese labourer asked her the same question.

Yolanda: I become very sad and angry hearing these. I even challenged a taxi driver on statistics, 'How many Indians have you met? If you haven't met a million of them, on what basis can you claim Indians are bad people?' But most of the time, I just walk away. There is a saying that one cannot wake up someone pretending to sleep. I can't show them the world if they prefer not to see it.

Shivaji: Generally, people in Singapore have mostly been amused, curious or pleased to see our coupling. Many say, 'Your children will be very good-looking,' 'You get to enjoy festivals from both sides,' 'Can you read or speak the other's language, show me?'

But things can change. During Covid and during the India–China border clashes, I came across so many anti-Chinese messages and memes. That makes me worried about going to India or Europe, or even Indonesia. Most people will certainly stay warm to us, but it only takes one crazy person to turn violent. I still get many anti-China WhatsApp forwards, some still naming Chinese people as viruses. I feel in two minds—are they harmless, or are they precursors to something nastier? So, should I object to these messages or just let them pass?

Being a mixed-race child, our daughter may indeed face some bullying or micro-aggressions in school. But what Yolanda and I can do is give her the confidence to face up to it. On the other hand, our child has the potential advantage of being able to converse, understand, and navigate the worlds of the two largest culture groups, Indian and Chinese. Perhaps she can be a citizen of the world who can overcome all boundaries with ease. We encourage her to pick up little bits of all cultures: a bit of

Balinese dance, some phrases in Khmer, a culinary experience in Vietnam. Maybe she can be free of all baggage that bind us but be loaded with all humanity's achievements that make us so magnificent.

I have been telling our daughter a bedtime story about the India–China war of 1962 and how my parents had little food back then. She has added new elements to this story herself, 'And then baba went to China and said that let's be friends. And then he met mama. And then they had a daughter— that's meee . . .'

Yolanda: And today, she asked, 'Why do China and India fight over the Himalayas? I will just build another Himalaya'

Photo Album

A collage of life in Indian–Chinese relationships in pictures.
Link: https://www.shivajidas.com/gallery

Acknowledgements

We are extremely thankful to all the individuals and couples who trusted us to share very personal stories. Writing a book of such scope would have been impossible without their selfless support in providing us with their precious time, understanding, and consideration. We are grateful for having forged many new friendships along this journey of writing this book. We are also grateful to all the social media communities for providing connections as well as other support: 'Chindian Diaries' Facebook page, 'Hakka from India' Facebook group, 'Chindian Club' Facebook group, 'Chinese Indian Association' Facebook group, 'Chinese daughters, Indian wives' WeChat group, and 'North American little groupie' WeChat group, etc.

We are deeply indebted to Kevin Bathman for his invaluable assistance and feedback at various stages of the book. We are immensely grateful to the team at Penguin Random House for their incredible support throughout the journey of this book, from conceptualization to its final form. In particular, we would like to thank Nora Nazerene Abu Bakar, for her round-the-clock support and timely interventions; Thatchaayanie Renganathan and Divya Vijayakumar, our editors, for their sharp pens; and Mr Gaurav Shrinagesh for having the confidence in us in developing this work.

Writing a book during the pandemic presented its own unique challenges, given that everyone's lives, including ours, were filled with many ups and downs. On that note, very special thanks from us to our four-year-old daughter, parents, extended families, and friends for constantly assuring us by providing a sense of normalcy while giving us the strength and confidence to pursue our initiative.